The Founder of Christianity

by the same author

C. H. Dodd

The Founder of
Christianity

COLLINS
St James's Place, London, 1971

First published in the United States of
America 1970 by The Macmillan Company, New
York, and in Canada by Collier-Macmillan
Canada Ltd., Toronto, Ontario

First published in Great Britain 1971
by William Collins Sons & Co. Ltd., London
First reprint 1971
Second reprint 1971
Third reprint 1971
Fourth reprint 1971
Fifth reprint 1972

ISBN 0 00 215257 6

CONTENTS

FOREWORD

It is a privilege to be invited by the British publisher to write a brief tribute to the author of this beautiful book. He needs of course no introduction from me or anyone else. As Director of the New English Bible, whose completion he has now lived to celebrate, Dr C. H. Dodd has already received in the Companionship of Honour from the Queen a token of the debt of gratitude owed him by the entire English-speaking world. It is indeed providential that this great enterprise should have been matched by a scholar whose profound learning has gone with such marvellous simplicity of thought and expression. Even King James's men had no such director – or the Authorized Version might have been less uneven than it is.

These qualities of scholarship and simplicity are strikingly revealed in this new book, which comes as freshly and as sharply from his mind as anything he has given us – despite the fact that he is now nearer ninety than eighty. Indeed, if the New English Bible represents the crown of his life's work, this could be said to be its distilled essence. It sometimes takes a professional scholar to appreciate just how good a popular book is. As a member once again of the Divinity Faculty at Cambridge where he taught I welcome this book, like so many others he has written, as one that could be put into the hands of any student or layman who knew nothing of the subject in the confidence that he would at once be able to understand and appreciate it.

Anyone acquainted with the history of "lives of Jesus" will know how mine-strewn an area this is. It takes confidence these days to venture into it at all. Yet the last three chapters of this book – "The Story" – reconstruct the essentials with a sureness of judgment and an economy of line that I found breathtaking. When others are popularizing portraits of Jesus (for instance, as a Zealot "freedom-fighter") which rest on assumption piled on dubious assumption, it is a relief to be able to recommend a study from a first-rate scholar – indeed *the* front-rank English-speaking New Testament scholar – that is solidly grounded as well as being eminently readable. This does not mean, of course, that all scholars will agree with everything in it. It does mean, I am confident, that all scholars will respect it.

In his inaugural lecture as Norris-Hulse Professor at Cambridge Dodd used these words: "The ideal interpreter would be one who has entered into that strange first-century world, has felt its whole strangeness, has sojourned in it until he has lived himself into it, thinking and feeling as one of those to whom the Gospel first came, and who will then return to our world, and give to the truth he has discerned a body out of the stuff of our own thought."

The journey of the biblical interpreter is (to quote the title of Dodd's delightful but little-known book of children's stories) *There and Back Again.* He has not been content to remain "there"; he has returned to our world and given what he has discerned a body out of the stuff of our thought.

At the beginning of that same inaugural of which I have just cited the conclusion occurs this portrait: "His weight of learning was worn lightly, and with an almost boyish freshness of mind . . . He was prodigal in sharing the resources of his knowledge and wisdom with others, and particularly with us younger men, who were stimulated by his unfailing zest for his subject, instructed by his mastery of method, and kept up to scratch by the example of his thoroughness, accuracy, and honesty of mind . . . His achievement remains, both as a sure foundation for further studies, and as an inspiration to those who labour at the same unending task."

That portrait was of his predecessor in the Chair, Professor F. C. Burkitt. But like a good painting, it tells us as much about the artist as it does of his sitter.

JOHN A. T. ROBINSON

PREFACE

The nucleus of this book was a course of four Syr. D. Owen Evans Lectures given in February 1954 at the University College of Wales, Aberystwyth. I am grateful to the College authorities both for the honour of their invitation and for their indulgence in allowing me to fulfill the requirement of publication by incorporating the substance of the lectures, with other material, in a forthcoming book. For various reasons publication has regrettably been delayed longer than was contemplated. In the interval the material of the lectures has been extensively reshaped and rewritten, though their broad pattern has been retained, and the proportion of added matter is considerable.

In quoting passages from the New Testament I have as a rule followed the translation in the New English Bible, © 1961, by kind permission of the publishers, the Oxford and Cambridge University presses, but occasionally I have preferred to give a rendering of my own.

C. H. DODD

Oxford, April 1969

I

INTRODUCTION

THE CHRISTIAN CHURCH is one of the facts of our time which one may like or dislike, but which no intelligent observer of the contemporary scene will wish to ignore. When therefore we set out to study the events out of which it arose, and the part that its Founder played in them, we are not like archaeologists digging up the remains of a forgotten civilization, or palaeontologists reconstructing an extinct organism. The events are part of the living fabric of a contemporary society whose dependence on its Founder is a permanent feature of its continuing existence. It may help to make this continuity more real to our minds if we attempt to trace, in barest outline, the place which the church has held in the history of the last nineteen centuries.

Putting the time-machine into reverse, we may find our first stopping place at the great upheaval of the sixteenth century which changed mediaeval Europe into the Europe that we know—or did know until the great wars once again moved the old landmarks. Humanism, Reformation, Counter-Reformation—these may stand for the forceful uprush of new ideas, which, with some unfortunate accompaniments, shaped a new world and inspired a new culture of which we became the heirs. The church stood near the center of the eruption, which indeed is not intelligible without it. The upheaval fragmented the church itself, and it still arouses passionate emotions in the fragments. Only a little reflection is needed to show that *that* part of its past at least is very much alive in the church of today. The present effort to transcend the divisions is one of the signs of its continued vitality.

Moving upstream, we come to the Middle Ages, the period of the gothic cathedrals, of the crusades, of great systems of law and administration, and of the massive scholastic philosophy. At that time Europe was "Christendom." Its civilization was directed by men who, however mistaken at times, intended to interpret and apply the principles of the Christian religion. Without the church, the Middle Ages would be a void.

Behind the Middle Ages lies the Dark Age, when Europe slowly struggled out of the mess into which it had been plunged by the decline of Rome and the incursions of the barbarians. The only institution which bridged the gap between the old civilization and the new one, as yet unborn, was the church. It preserved the rudiments of law, order and humanity. It encouraged, through the monastic orders, the revival of agriculture and crafts, and it laid the foundations of learning and education. It is impossible to conceive what would have come out of the chaos of the Dark Age without the church.

On the far side of the gap lay the Roman Empire, the final embodiment of the older civilization. Under Constantine the Great, Rome accepted the leadership of the Christian Church, which gradually took the whole system under its guidance, to hand on its most vital elements to a later age. The persecution to which Constantine put an end had been a matter of survival. The church prevailed not only because it had the faith, tenacity and courage to survive, but also because it had proved itself superior to its rivals.

Behind Constantine lay two centuries and a half of struggle. At times it was overt, often it was concealed; but at no time was any emperor free from anxiety about the "Christian question." At an early stage of the struggle, two Roman writers have left a record of the way in which they looked at the "Christian question" of their time.

Early in the second century the Roman governor of the province of Bithynia in Asia Minor, Gaius Plinius Secundus, commonly called the Younger Pliny, wrote to the Emperor Trajan about some of his problems.[1] He had on his hands strikes, municipal scandals, and political disaffection. There was also some religious unrest. Many temples, he reported, were practically deserted, and in some, services had been discontinued. There was a slump in agricultural markets, because people were no longer buying beasts for sacrifice as they should. It was all the fault, so his informants said, of some people called "Christians," who formed a secret society which could be up to no good, and who were certainly disloyal to the empire, since they refused to offer sacrifice to the god-emperor. So a number of Christians were arrested and brought to trial. The examination (according to the governor's report) failed to find evidence against the accused of any criminal activities. At worst, it pointed to "a degraded and extravagant superstition." But they did refuse sacrifice to the emperor, and anyhow they deserved to be punished for their "inflexible obstinacy."

In the course of the examination, Pliny found out

something about the practices of the Christian society. They were accustomed, he discovered, to meet
on a fixed day very early in the morning, to sing
hymns responsively to Christ "as to a god," and to
bind themselves by a solemn oath, not (as he had
apparently expected) to some nefarious crime, but to
keep the moral law: not to rob or steal, not to
commit adultery, not to defraud. Later, they took a
meal together, a very simple and harmless meal (the
governor notes)—and nothing more. Pliny is a bit confused about what actually happened when Christians
met on Sunday, but there is not much difficulty in re-
cognizing some of the elements of what is now called
a Communion Service.   Millions of people all over
the world took part in just such a service last Sunday.

    That was in A.D. 112. About that time a friend of
Pliny's, Cornelius Tacitus, was engaged on a history
of the Rome of the Emperors.[2] He came to the reign
of Nero, and to the great fire of Rome. Rumors had
got about that the emperor had had a hand in starting the fire. Something must be done, so the Roman
police looked about for a scapegoat. They found
one, says Tacitus, in a body of people known as
"Christians," who were generally disliked by the
Roman populace for their disgraceful practices. So a
number of Christians were arrested and charged with
arson. Many were put to death, with such refine-
ments of torture that public dislike began to turn
to sympathy for the victims. Tacitus does not appear
to believe the charge of incendiarism, but he com-
ments brutally that they were anyhow enemies of
society (and so by implication deserved what they
got). Their founder, he learned, was a criminal who
had been executed by Pontius Pilate, governor of
Judaea, thirty years or so earlier. Unfortunately the
death of the ringleader had not stopped the mischief.

The "pestilent superstition" had flared out again, and soon reached Rome, where, he bitterly remarks, every foul and horrible thing finds its way sooner or later. At the time of the fire, its adherents amounted to an "immense multitude"; so he says, but possibly he exaggerates the danger to society. So here at last, from a reputable, if unamiable, Roman historian, we have an account of the beginnings of Christianity, in the late twenties or early thirties of the first century.

Our journey upstream has brought us to a highly significant period in the history of the world. The Roman Empire had recently taken shape under Augustus (whose reign spans the transition from "B.C." to "A.D."). It was an immense political achievement. It also made possible new adventures of the human spirit, for it was like a great reservoir into which the currents of ancient civilization flowed, and out of which rose all the streams of later history in the western world. In the spiritual sphere, quite apart from Christianity, it saw the harvesting of earlier tendencies in the emergence of new ways of religion and a new outlook in philosophy. Tacitus could not know, nor Pliny, that the group of people whom the one thought a danger to society and the other a set of pig-headed cranks were the vanguard of a body which would take charge of the whole new movement, give it direction, and carry it into ages far ahead. But so it was. Among numerous new faiths with which the Roman Empire abounded, *one* was destined to survive, carrying the germ of a new order —the Christian religion, whose Founder, born under Augustus, was put to death under his successor Tiberius; and whose followers, soon becoming a large and influential society, paid him divine honors and vowed themselves to him for the service of the moral law.

It is now time to look at the origins of this society at closer range. Judaea, says Tacitus, was the place where the trouble began, so to Judaea we must now direct our attention. Palestine lay near the eastern confines of the Roman Empire, which in that region was the successor of the Greek monarchies set up after Alexander the Great had conquered the Persians. Throughout the region, the Greek language and Greek culture were a binding force, while political unity was imposed by the Roman administration. Most of the subject peoples were reasonably content to have it so. Roman rule might be severe, often harsh, sometimes oppressive, but it was an improvement on the anarchy and misrule of the Greek monarchies in their decline. Palestine, however, was an exception. The Jews who formed the dominant part of its population were a peculiar and a stubborn people. The Romans never understood them. They had for long been subjects, first of the Persian Empire and then of the Greek monarchies of Syria and Egypt. They had absorbed a good deal of the culture of their successive masters, but a nationalist revival in the second century B.C. had given them a taste of independence under a native dynasty. It began in the heroic resistance of the Maccabees, flourished for a time under their successors, the Hasmonaean princes, and fizzled out in sordid squabbles among their last heirs, when a Roman takeover became inevitable. But the Jews did not forget their brief spell of glory, and indulged a dangerous nostalgia. The first intention of the Romans had been to govern by "indirect rule," and for a time it worked, but in the end the southern part of the country was organized as the Roman province of Judaea, under governors of secondary rank with the title of prefect (subsequently procurator), while the rest was left under puppet princes. At the time of our story the prefect of Judaea was Pontius Pilate, whose term of office was from A.D. 26 to 37.

North of Judaea proper, but still within the Roman province, was the district known as Samaria. Its inhabitants were of Israelite and mixed descent, and followed a religion basically the same as that of the Jews, though it deviated in some particulars. But the Jews ostracized them as aliens and heretics. Rankling memories of the past, and centuries of estrangement, had bred between these people of kindred stock, close neighbors in a very small country, a mentality of mutual hatred, which found expression constantly in petty provocations and occasionally in murderous affrays.

The northern part of Palestine, known as Galilee, with the territory to the east of the Jordan, was under a native prince, Herod Antipas. Galilee had a mixed population, thick on the ground. It was a hotbed of Jewish disaffection. Many Galileans who passed for Jews must have been descended from foreigners forcibly "converted" when the Hasmonaean princes conquered the territory, but their zeal for their religion was not the less fanatical for that. The prefect of Judaea always kept an anxious eye on the turbulent Galileans who descended in their thousands on Jerusalem for the national religious festivals. At such seasons he was accustomed to leave the seat of government at Caesarea and take up residence in Jerusalem, and to see that an adequate force of troops was on hand in the castle overlooking the temple courts.

For the temple was the nerve center of Jewish life. Politically, the tiny Jewish enclave was negligible, but as a religious center it had world-wide significance.

B

Of this the Roman government was well aware, for there were Jews everywhere in the empire who looked to Jerusalem as their metropolis. Five centuries earlier, when the Jewish community revived after having been almost extinguished as a separate entity, it had organized itself as something more like a church than a state. Its "constitution" (if we may call it so), at least as fundamental and immutable as that of the United States, was the so-called Law of Moses, which not only covered the field of civil and ecclesiastical order, but also provided a comprehensive code of social and personal ethics by which, in theory, every member of the community, whether resident in the mother country or dispersed abroad, was bound. In consequence, that class of persons who were recognized as learned in the Law, and made it their business to expound it, acquired a position of peculiar influence and prestige. These persons were known by a term which is conventionally translated as "scribes," but might be more adequately represented by some such phrase as "doctors of the Law." The obvious difficulty of carrying out the provisions of the Law in all their minutiae, in a situation far more complicated than that for which they were originally framed, led those who desired seriously to make the attempt to form themselves into "fellowships" for mutual support and instruction. The members of these fellowships had come to be known, in our period, as "Pharisees," a word of uncertain derivation, which is thought to mean something like "the separated." If so, it would describe their position aptly enough, for they evidently felt themselves, and other people felt them, to be in some measure separate from "the people who care nothing for the Law." They were respected and influential, and their fellowships included men of high moral and intellectual quality, though they were no doubt open to the temptations common to people who set out to be more religious than their neighbors. They were strong in the local "synagogues," which served not only as places of worship but as social centers and even, to a limited extent, as organs of local self-government for the Jewish 'community.

In the capital, the presence of the temple gave overriding power and prestige to the hierarchy. The High Priest, whose office was hereditary in certain families, exercised great authority, though the Romans had clipped his wings considerably. He presided over the grand council or senate, known as the Sanhedrin (a Greek word spelled as Hebrew— a sign of the depth to which Greek influence had penetrated). The imperial authorities, after their custom in the provinces, allowed the Sanhedrin to exercise a substantial, though well controlled, measure of local autonomy. In the main the priestly aristocracy and their immediate adherents tended to be friendly, or subservient, to the Romans. It was to their interest, and they may well have believed it was to the interest of Jewry as a whole, to maintain as smooth relations with the paramount power as was possible in the situation. At the time of our story the High Priest was Joseph Caiaphas, who had been put into the office by Pilate's predecessor. But much power seems to have remained in the hands of his father-in-law, Annas. Annas had been induced or forced to retire from the highest office some years earlier, but it was only to remain influential behind the scenes while he maneuvered five of his sons in succession, as well as his son-in-law, on to the pontifical throne. The "house of Annas" has an unsavory reputation in Jewish tradition.

Some of the most potent elements, however, in Jewish society of the first century stood outside the official establishment. There were various sects with their own peculiar doctrines and practices. One of these has in recent years become known to us through the discovery of the so-called "Dead Sea Scrolls." These contain the sectarian literature of a quasi-monastic community whose settlement has been identified at a spot known as Qumran. While fanatically zealous for the Law they had their own interpretation of its precepts. They repudiated the priesthood in Jerusalem, in favor of priests of their own, whose "orders" (to use modern phraseology) they regarded as alone "valid." They guarded an exclusive membership and lived under a strict and puritanical discipline, practicing rituals of the most demanding kind. They were ferociously nationalist in temper. One of their documents contains elaborate directions for the organization of an army to fight against the "Sons of Darkness." It moves largely in the realms of fantasy, but there is no reason to doubt that these sectaries did look forward to a final war of liberation ending with the triumph of the Jewish people over all their enemies. The document does not mention the Romans by name but their alias is sufficiently transparent.

Whether the pious sectaries contemplated turning fantasy into reality by joining in a military rising is uncertain. Probably they did. If they did not, there were others who did. Ever since, in A.D. 6, a certain Judas of Galilee had led an abortive rising against the Roman government, an underground resistance movement remained in being, and broke out sporadically from time to time, until at last they succeeded in precipitating a full-scale rebellion in A.D. 66. They liked to be called Zealots. The government called them bandits. The type is familiar enough in the twentieth century. The attitude of the Pharisees toward this clandestine movement seems to have been equivocal; many of them would probably have said that they approved their aims but disapproved of their methods. The priestly aristocrats were nervously anxious to damp down any dangerous manifestation of militant nationalism.

Altogether, what with party rivalries, sectarian disputes and political differences, Palestine in the first half of the first century was in a state of constant unsettlement. It was in this atmosphere of tension that, as Jewish tradition avers, "they hanged Jesus of Nazareth on the Eve of Passover because he practiced sorcery and was leading Israel astray." [3] It is as unsympathetic an account as the Roman historian's, but once again it is an outside view which helps to put the beginnings of Christianity on the map of first-century history.

That is about as far as we can get by looking at the matter from the outside. It is now time to take a fresh look from the inside.

Once again, we may start with contemporary facts, under our immediate observation, and move upstream. If we want to get an inside view of the Christian movement, the natural course is to go into the church—any church. What are these people doing? The church does a good many things, some of them perhaps more useful and relevant than others. Some of them are being done by other bodies— better done, it may be. But there is one activity in which the church meets with no competition. Its special business is the worship of God. Let us assume, at least for the purpose of argument, that worship is a serious employment for intelligent be-

ings, and worth trying to understand. Unless we do
in some measure understand it, we are not likely to
understand either the nature or the history of the
church. That assumption being granted, it is in-
teresting to ask what exactly Christians do in church
when they worship God. I am not here asking about
the fathomless profundities of man's communion
with the Deity, but about what anyone may observe
when Christians are engaged in worship.

Their ways of worship vary a good deal; but in
any church you may enter you will find that certain
things always form part of it. They all make use of
some form of words, spoken or sung, which express
belief in God. They praise God for his goodness and
power, and thank him for all good things of life, because they believe him to be the Maker of all things,
visible and invisible. Thinking of his goodness, and
of all that seems to deny that goodness, they confess
their own misdeeds, follies and weaknesses, ask for
and accept forgiveness and offer themselves to his
service. Again, since God is the source of all good,
they ask him for things desirable and necessary for
themselves and for other people. They also listen
while passages are read from the Bible, a collection
of ancient writings of various kinds, in which the
being and attributes of God are set forth in many
different aspects and the moral law is declared; in
which also events of ancient times are recorded. This
preoccupation with ancient history is a characteristic,
and at first sight a rather curious, feature of Christian worship. Many people have no patience with it,
and ask, what have all these bygones to do with the
needs of people in the twentieth century? Part of the
answer is that these ancient events are moments in a
living process which includes also the existence of
the church at the present day; and another part is

that, as Christians believe, in these events of ancient
time God was at work among men, and it is from his
action in history rather than from abstract argu-
ments that we learn what God is like, and what are
the principles on which he deals with men, now as
always. In any case, it was out of these events that
the church itself emerged, and this, they believe, was
God's doing. If we are enquiring into the historical
origins of Christianity, this testimony to events is of
considerable interest.

Among the services of the church there is one in
particular which in different forms is observed by all
kinds of Christian societies. It is variously known as
the sacrament of the Lord's Supper, or Holy Communion, or the Eucharist, or the Mass. Under all its
different forms we can recognize features of the
Sunday assembly of Christians which intrigued the
Roman Pliny in A.D. 112. As then, so now, the assembly of Christians is centered on a communal meal
—reduced now to its simplest elements of bread and
wine. About that central act cluster most of the
elements of Christian worship which we have briefly
noted. At the crucial point of the service you will
hear spoken some such words as these:

> The Lord Jesus, on the night of his arrest, took
> bread, and after giving thanks to God, broke it
> and said: "This is my body, which is for you; do
> this as a memorial of me." In the same way, he took
> the cup after supper, and said, "This cup is the
> new covenant sealed by my blood. Whenever you
> drink it, do this as a memorial of me."

When these words are spoken, it is understood that
the whole service is placed within the context of
what Jesus said, did, and suffered on the occasion
referred to, and is to be understood on that basis.

The depth of meaning which Christian people find in those words it is not necessary here to attempt to set forth. But it is important, for our present purpose, to observe that in this central act of Christian worship—in this act, therefore, which more than any other expresses all that Christianity is—there is included an act of remembrance. The church—every gathering of the church, everywhere, under every form—*remembers* that on a certain night its Founder said and did certain definite things, briefly reported; that on the same night he fell into the hands of his enemies; and that he suffered a violent death (for the broken body and the shed blood can mean nothing else). The memory of the church thus takes us back to the same point where we formerly dropped anchor on our journey up the stream of history— the moment of the foundation of the church, when its Founder "suffered under Pontius Pilate." All lines run back to that precise point, which we might date tentatively to Friday, April 7, A.D. 30. Not indeed that the exact calendar date is either certain or important; other dates are possible between A.D. 29 and 33; but it *is* of some importance that the church remembers an event which is actual, concrete and in principle dateable like any other historical event.

The remembrance goes back in a continuous chain. At every service there are present elderly people who fifty or sixty years ago heard those words spoken by, or in the presence of, men old enough to be their grandparents; there are young people who, it may be, will repeat them in the hearing of their grandchildren. And so the endless chain goes on. For nineteen centuries there has not been one single week in which this act of remembrance was not made, one generation reminding another.

This continuity of memory within the church may

be illustrated by an example. Round about A.D. 200
there died at Lyons in France the bishop of that
city, Irenaeus by name, one of the outstanding Christian leaders of his time. It happens that a letter of
his has come down to us, addressed to an old fellow
student named Florinus from whom he had been
separated for many years. The letter brings up reminiscences of their student days together at the city
of Smyrna in Asia Minor. In particular he recalls
how they used to attend lectures by Polycarp, bishop
of Smyrna, who died about A.D. 155, at the age of at
least eighty-six. He must have been getting on in
years when Irenaeus and Florinus heard him. Irenaeus reminds his old companion—and there would
have been no point in it if Florinus could not con-
firm his recollections—how Polycarp used to tell
them stories about "John the disciple of the Lord,"
whom he had known personally many years before.
Which of the persons named John was meant, seems
uncertain, but that he was a personal follower of
Jesus is clear. Irenaeus, then, in France shortly before
A.D. 200, was able to recall at only one remove a
man who had known Jesus intimately. When the
bishop of Lyons broke bread with his little congre-
gation as a memorial of the death of Jesus, he was
not thinking of something he had found (where Kip-
ling's John Nicholson found his God) "in a printed
book," but of something that he had been told by his
old teacher, whose friend had been there and knew.
That is what the memory of the church is like.

A corporate memory handed down from generation to generation becomes what we call a tradition.
Our knowledge about the origins of the church, and
about its Founder, rests primarily on a living tradition, which had its beginnings in the actual memories of those who had witnessed the events and had

personal dealings with the principal Actor in them.

A tradition may be altered or distorted in the course of long transmission by word of mouth. When once it is written, it stands substantially unaltered. It may therefore be tested and controlled by a careful and critical study of the documents which caught and fixed it at the earliest accessible stage in its development. The New Testament contains the deposit, in writing, of the continuous tradition about Jesus at various stages of its transmission during the first century of the church's existence. The principal documents are the four gospels, and to these we must now turn. Meanwhile it is a fact of some significance that these records, whatever their historical value in detail, are about a Person whose role in history was *remembered*. For the event to which we have been led back by all lines of approach, from outside and from inside, is not some remote, forgotten episode of the past, recovered, as it might be, through digging up an ancient tomb or unearthing a manuscript in a cave. It is something that has never dropped out of the memory of the oldest surviving societies in the western world.

II

THE DOCUMENTS

THE NEW TESTAMENT contains at least one book which is offered to the reader as an historical composition in the full sense. It is a history of the Beginnings of Christianity, in two parts or volumes. Volume I we know as the Gospel according to Luke, Volume II as the Acts of the Apostles. The date of the two-volume work is uncertain; presumably some time elapsed between the publication of the two parts. If we take A.D. 75 and 95 as the outside limits, we shall probably not go far wrong. The author has been identified, from the time when the New Testament writings were first collected, as the Greek physician Luke who was for some years on the "staff" of the apostle Paul, and this may be right. Of his aim and method he has told us something in an "epistle dedicatory" addressed to a person of high rank named Theophilus, of whom nothing further is known. He writes as follows:

Many writers have undertaken to draw up an account of the events that have happened among us, following the traditions handed down to us by

17

the original eyewitnesses and servants of the gospel. And so I in my turn, your Excellency, as one who has gone over the whole course of these events in detail, have decided to write a connected narrative for you, so as to give you authentic knowledge about the matters of which you have been informed.[1]

It was a literary convention of the period to introduce an historical work in some such way, but it is of course possible to conform to a literary convention and yet to speak the truth. Obviously, by introducing his work in this way Luke means it to be taken as an historical work. It seems fair to assume that he writes in good faith, whatever may be thought of his competence as an historian. We may take it then that he was acquainted with a tradition handed down from eyewitnesses and of written narratives based upon it. He claims to have undertaken an independent investigation—dealing, we infer, both with the oral tradition and with the documentary sources —and to have made out of his findings a connected narrative. This claim we have no reason to doubt. Critical analysis confirms that both written sources and oral tradition have entered into the composition, but that the continuity has, in both volumes, been largely supplied by the author. His intelligent efforts to produce a satisfactory chronological scheme have met with much difficulty and less than complete success.

Of his written sources one at least can be identified with certainty. It is no other than our Gospel according to Mark, to which we must give attention presently. To this source Luke owes a large part of his narrative (as distinct from his report of the teaching of Jesus), and he usually, though not always, prefers it to the other "accounts of the events" with

which he was acquainted, and which he has sometimes followed. A substantial part of his report of the
sayings of Jesus (as distinct from the narrative) is
closely parallel, sometimes even verbally identical,
with the report given in the Gospel according to
Matthew. To the latter work we must now turn.

It is in certain ways strikingly different from the
Gospel according to Luke. Its author never comes
before us in person, as Luke does. He tells us nothing
about his purpose or his procedure, or about the
sources to which he went for information. While
Luke's history is an individual venture, Matthew's
work appears to be something more like an officially
sponsored textbook for the instruction of converts
to the church. Its date cannot be determined, nor is
there any wide agreement about it among critics,
but it is (in my judgment) not likely to be any earlier
than Luke's history of the Beginnings. The name of
Matthew has always been attached to it, but it is improbable that the apostle of that name was its author,
though he may well have sponsored some of the
material it embodies. For narrative it depends almost
exclusively on Mark. But the interest of the work is
centered much more on the report of the sayings of
Jesus. Here it is richer than Luke, and the material
is far more elaborately organized, obviously with an
eye to its effective use for teaching.

If we enquire after the sources from which the
author derived the sayings, the answer must depend
on minute critical analysis, and is never likely to be
more than probable. It seems that he drew from a
variety of sources, written or oral, and that he has
edited them more or less. One thing, however, we can
say with reasonable certainty is that the large body
of sayings which he gives in common with Luke must
have come down to both, whether in writing or by

word of mouth, from a period much earlier than the date at which the two authors wrote.[2] It brings us that much nearer to the fountainhead.

It is thus to Matthew and Luke that we look for our fullest report of the teaching of Jesus, and it will be convenient to give some attention to this before turning to the narrative. What is the character of this report, and how did it come to be compiled?

The early church was a society which did its business in the world chiefly through the living voice, in preaching, teaching and worship. And it was mainly through the living voice that the sayings of Jesus were first handed down. From the way in which Paul introduces sayings which he quotes in his letters we should conjecture that he knew them from word of mouth rather than in writing, though some of them may already have been written down, if only by way of *aide-memoire* for the convenience of teachers. At any rate by the date at which Paul was writing—say, some quarter of a century after the death of Jesus— there was already in circulation a body of accepted "sayings of the Lord" to which he could appeal in the confidence that his correspondents would acknowledge their authority. That collections of such sayings should be made—some here, some there, by various persons—to serve the practical needs of the church, was in the nature of things, and these collections of sayings provided the gospel writers with much of their raw material.

Oral tradition is a somewhat precarious vehicle. Memory can play tricks; many a slip is possible between the hearing of a thing and its repetition to another person. True; but there are some considerations to be set against this. The earliest Christians were Jews. Among Jews of that period it was well understood that a disciple was responsible for remembering and faithfully handing on the teaching of his master. We need not suppose that the disciples of Jesus were either less conscientious or less competent than the disciples of other teachers. The question, indeed, whether we have his very words is one which, put in that form, cannot be answered. He spoke in Aramaic; we have his sayings in a Greek translation, made, presumably, by bilingual Christians who did their best to give the sense. We sometimes find different attempts to translate the same saying. Nor, so far as we can judge, was the same stress laid upon word-for-word repetition as in the Jewish schools. Those through whom the tradition came down were practical teachers. They were concerned to carry the meaning across to their hearers. They might recast a saying to make it more directly applicable to the existing situation, which might be unlike that in which the words were spoken. Or they might insert an explanatory comment, and the comment would come to form part of the tradition. Or again, contemporary debate with the non-Christian public they wished to win, or even within the Christian community itself, might lead them to a possibly unbalanced elaboration of certain aspects of the sayings. But the intention was always to hand on what Jesus himself taught, and to bring this home to the hearers or readers.

When all allowance has been made for these limiting factors—the chances of oral transmission, the effect of translation, the interest of teachers in making the sayings "contemporary," and simple human fallibility—it remains that the first three gospels offer a body of sayings on the whole so consistent, so coherent, and withal so distinctive in manner, style content, that no reasonable critic should doubt, whatever reservations he may have about individual sayings, that we find reflected here the thought of a single, unique teacher.

To assume that these gospels give us a complete and rounded picture of the teaching of Jesus on all its sides would perhaps be going too far. A different angle is adopted in a work of which nothing has yet been said, the Gospel according to John. This has always been held to be the latest of the four, though it is perhaps the latest by a margin so narrow as to have little significance. It was brought out, in all probability, not far from A.D. 100, possibly on the earlier side. In antiquity it was believed to have been written by John son of Zebedee, one of the inner circle of the disciples of Jesus. It may be so, but there are serious difficulties in the way of accepting his authorship. What is clear is that this gospel is more of an original composition than the others. Its style has an individuality of its own, which is clearly that of the author rather than of Jesus himself. In selecting matter to be included in his work he was guided by the needs and interests of the public for which he wrote. So indeed were the others; but his was the cosmopolitan and cultivated public of a great Greek city; the book was in all probability produced at Ephesus.

In presenting the teaching of Jesus he employed a method familiar to educated Greek readers. It began with Plato, who presented the teaching of his master Socrates through dialogues which are his own composition, in his own inimitable style, and yet have given to succeeding ages a convincing picture of that remarkable man. The "set pieces" of the Fourth Gospel, composed with great art, are comparable with the Greek philosophical dialogue. Yet dispersed among these elaborate literary compositions, or even embedded in them, there are sayings which stand out because they have the familiar ring. Some indeed are recognizably identical with sayings reported in the other gospels, though the wording may differ because the writer has his own linguistic habits, and sometimes he gives what seems to be a different translation of the same Aramaic original. In addition, on a closer examination of the dialogues and discourses it often turns out that the writer is only spelling out, in his own idiom of thought, what is already implicit in sayings reported in the other gospels. All this encourages the belief that the writer drew from the same general reservoir of tradition. That reservoir, we may be sure, contained more than has come through in our written gospels. There are sayings of Jesus recorded only in the Fourth Gospel which seem to bring into relief aspects of his teachings slenderly represented, if at all, in the others, and these may be of importance to complete the picture. It would be unwise to neglect them, though to make use of them in a strictly historical investigation calls for some critical tact.

So far our attention has been concentrated on the gospel record of the *teaching* of Jesus. It would have been possible for this teaching to be put before the public in the form of a collection of sayings. There are in fact such collections known to us, though of somewhat later date, and it is probable, as we have seen, that similar collections lay before the writers of the gospels. But it is evident that these did not satisfy the demands of the Christian community, for the four writings which were selected as authoritative have the character of *narratives* into which sayings are inserted at suitable or significant points. We must now consider the narrative constituent of the gospels.

c

Our natural starting point will be the Gospel according to Mark, which provides the main basis of the narrative in Matthew and Luke. It is probably to be dated between A.D. 65 and 70, or thereabouts—just about the time when the first generation of Christians was dying off, but when many who remembered the events must still have been alive. Whether Mark was one of these we cannot say; he may have been, but in any case there is little in his book to suggest that he had been a witness of the events he records. An examination of his work suggests that he was less of an author and more of a compiler than the others. That is to say, he appears to have reproduced what came down to him with comparatively little attempt to write it up in his own way, unlike Luke, who composes with an eye to literary effect and with an effort to give some semblance of chronological continuity, and unlike Matthew, who presents his material with a sure pedagogical touch. In Mark, within a very broad general scheme, there is a certain freedom and looseness of arrangement, and in his rather rough and informal style we seem often to overhear the tones of the living voice telling a story. We are probably near to the "original eyewitnesses and servants of the gospel" to whom Luke refers. By "servants of the gospel" he means Christian missionaries who spread the faith in the earliest days. In defining the contents of his book as "The Gospel of Jesus Christ," rather than "Memoirs of Jesus" or the like, Mark has made it clear that he conceives himself as continuing, through the medium of writing, the same work which the missionaries were doing through the living voice. Elsewhere in the New Testament the term "gospel" always means the Christian message as preached; its now familiar use, as meaning a book about Jesus,

developed later, and Mark was very likely responsible, indirectly, for this development.

The manner in which the "servants of the gospel"
communicated their message may be gathered from
the abridged specimens of early Christian preaching
which Luke has supplied in his second volume.[3]
They are represented as declaring (to summarize
with impossible brevity) that the divinely guided
history of Israel has reached a climax of "fulfilment."
A new era has dawned; a community has come into
existence—in effect a new Israel—in which there is
offered forgiveness for the past, spiritual power for
the present, and hope for the future. It has its creative center in the Messiah whom God has sent, and
this is no other than Jesus of Nazareth, recently crucified and now risen from the dead. Thus the whole
tremendous crisis is linked with the historical career
of Jesus, and it becomes important to have some
trustworthy knowledge of this. Mark has set out to
provide what is required. The themes of the preaching are there: the note of "fulfilment," the emergence of a community, the offer of forgiveness, the
outlook on the future, the whole receiving its im-
pulse from Jesus, what he said, what he did, what
happened to him. Mark is preaching the gospel;
he is doing it by telling a story belonging to the
world of actual fact: the world in which Herod Antipas and Pontius Pilate played the parts on the public stage which secular historians ascribe to them;
the world in which the machinery of Roman rule
operated in ways known to all students of the period;
the world which was disturbed by the familiar tensions and conflicts of the last half century of the
Jewish state.

There is thus a double strain in his work. It contains a report of certain happenings, together with,

and inseparably interwoven with, an interpretation of these happenings. The same double strain, fact *plus* interpretation, reappears in Matthew and Luke. The three differ in some matters of factual detail, and to some extent in the way in which they express the significance they attach to the events; but the differences are not of substance. In the Fourth Gospel, interpretation is more deliberate and self-conscious, and it employs more sophisticated theological concepts. These concepts are in part derived from a religious philosophy widely current at the time in the Greek-speaking East, though here they come out very differently. Essentially, however, all four gospels alike have the character of fact *plus* interpretation.

The tension between these two constituents of the narrative has provided much of the interest of critical debate upon the gospels during the last century or more. And indeed there has been, and is, a similar debate among secular historiographers, and the phases through which criticism has passed have to a striking degree kept pace in the biblical and the secular fields. In the nineteenth century (which for this purpose as for many others ended in 1914), critics tended on the whole to say: strip off the interpretation so far as possible; it only tells us what some early Christians thought or believed; the residue will be plain matter of fact. The trouble was that as criticism refined its methods while following its own logic the area of what could be accepted as sheer, uninterpreted matter of fact shrank almost to nothing. It was, as one of them said, like peeling an onion. So in the present century many critics have said, in effect: let us look again at what we discarded. It may not have much value as evidence for the facts of the life of Jesus, but it is at any rate undeniable first-hand evidence for the faith of the early church, and this is well worth studying. So indeed it is. The turnabout did much to revivify gospel criticism, which, to tell the truth, had grown somewhat stale. But some of the new criticism went so far as to say that the gospels can give us *nothing but* the ideas of early Christians. They do not convey information about Jesus himself as he lived; that was something to which their authors were indifferent; they meant to produce religious, not historical, documents.

This was an overstatement of an important truth which had been sometimes rather overlooked. The gospels are indeed religious documents; they do bear witness to the faith of the church; but that is not to say that they are not also historical documents or that their authors had no interest in the facts. Unless Luke is grossly misleading his readers, he set out, like his predecessors in the field, "to draw up an account of the events that have happened," in order to convey authentic knowledge about them. And since he treated Mark as a valuable, though by no means an infallible, source of information, we may take it that he regarded Mark as an historical as well as a religious document; and it seems impossible to deny a similar character to the other two gospels as well.

The truth is that the attempt to make a sharp division between fact and interpretation and set them over against one another is misguided, whether it takes the form of seeking to establish the facts by eliminating the interpretation, or of attending exclusively to interpretation, and dismissing the question of fact as irrelevant. To the serious historian (as distinct from the mere chronicler) the interest and meaning which an event bore for those who felt its impact is a part of the event. This is now widely recognized in secular historiography. But it is of peculiar significance in a Christian context. In the Hebrew-Christian type of religion, events are held to be the medium through which God discloses his ways to men. This is the belief that runs all through the Old Testament. In the New Testament the divine disclosure is held to be made supremely in what Luke calls "the facts about Jesus." [4]

These facts are communicated with the intention of bringing out as forcibly as possible the meaning which our authors believed to be their true meaning. In that sense the gospels are an expression of the faith of the church. The hinge on which that faith turned was the belief that Jesus, having been put to death by crucifixion, "rose from the dead." This is not a belief that grew up within the church, or a doctrine whose development might be traced. It is the central belief about which the church itself grew, without which there would have been no church and no gospels, at least of the kind we have. So much the historian must affirm; upon the truth or falsity of the belief he is not obliged, or indeed entitled, to pronounce. About this belief in the resurrection of Jesus more will have to be said later, but for our present purpose it is important to note that the various stories about the "appearances" of the risen Christ to his followers—which differ considerably in the several gospels and perhaps cannot be fully harmonized—have one constant feature in common. They clearly do not refer to anything in the nature of a vague "mystical experience"; they are all centered in a moment of *recognition*. You cannot recognize a person unless you remember him. Thus an act of remembrance—the remembrance of a real

and well-known person—is a built-in feature of the
faith that inspired the writing of the gospels. For
the original "eyewitnesses and servants of the gospel," the memory was quite recent. But it was a
memory now illuminated by a discovery that left
them at first gasping with astonishment: that the
Leader they had thought irretrievably lost had got
the better of death itself, in a way as inexplicable as
it was indubitable. So at least they believed, and it
put the whole story in a new light. Thus the gospels
record remembered facts, but record them as understood on the farther side of resurrection. There is no
reason why this should be supposed to falsify or dis-
tort the record, unless, of course, it be assumed at
the outset that such a belief *cannot* be true. Short of
this, it is legitimate to recall that "hindsight" often
gives a clue to happenings which at the time did not
make sense. In the gospels we are not infrequently
told that not only the general public, but his own
followers, failed to understand some things that Jesus
said and did. The implication is that now they did
understand; and that seems reasonable enough.

But if this is so, there is something more to be
said. If the resurrection is the true dénouement
of the whole story and not a "happy ending" tacked
on to a tragedy, then there is an element in the story
itself which brings us to the frontiers of normal human experience, where experience runs out into mystery. It is a story about things that actually happened, but in the light of the sequel they have an
extra dimension. Such a story could not be told
wholly in terms of matter of fact, in straight, literal
prose. It required the aid of symbolism and imagery.
For this purpose the narrators had at their disposal
an inherited stock of images and symbols derived
largely from Jewish poetry and prophecy. This de-

termines the idiom in which the story is told, an idiom not merely of language but of thought and even of feeling, with which the reader needs to put himself in sympathy.

The author of the Fourth Gospel, at the point at which he is about to launch out upon his account of the public career of Jesus, tells his readers what they are to look out for: "You will see heaven wide open, and God's angels ascending and descending upon the Son of Man." [5] John does not mean that he is going to describe a scene in which winged beings are visibly flying up and down; there is no such scene in the gospels. He means that in the whole story, and in each item of it, the discerning reader will perceive a traffic between two worlds. He will read how in this unique career heaven and earth, God and man, were brought together as nowhere else.

But this symbolism could also be used in the description of particular occurrences. Not only in John but in all the gospels, with slight variations, we read that when Jesus was baptized "he saw the heavens torn wide open and the Spirit like a dove descending upon him," while a voice spoke from heaven. It is idle to ask what actually happened, if by that you mean, what was there that might have been photographed on film or recorded on tape, had such convenient facilities been available. But in a deeper and more real sense "what actually happened" on this occasion was something very important indeed. It was, as we say, an "historic occasion." It was a turning point in the career of Jesus himself, and a crucial moment in that traffic of two worlds of which John spoke. Its profound significance could be suggested only by the use of the most solemn and impressive imagery.

Symbols and images of this kind cluster thickly in

the scenes of the "Christmas story" which in Matthew and Luke is the prelude to their account of the public career of Jesus: visits of angels, prophetic dreams, the marvelous star in the east, the miraculous birth greeted with songs from the heavenly choir, all the appealing incidents so familiar in the appropriate setting of Christmas carol and nativity play. That there is a basis of fact somewhere behind it all need not be doubted, but he would be a bold man who should presume to draw a firm line between fact and symbol. What our authors are saying through all this structure of imagery is that the obscure birth of a child to a carpenter's wife was, in view of all that came out of it, a decisive moment in history, when something genuinely new began, and the traffic of two worlds was initiated, to be traced by the discerning eye all through the story that was to follow.

This use of symbolism is fundamentally poetical. It is not a flight into fantasy. It means that the facts are being viewed in depth, not superficially. This must be taken into account when we consider the stories of miracles which have so large a place in some parts of the gospels. In the Fourth Gospel these are treated frankly as "signs," that is, symbols. Not that John thought they did not happen, but their happening was of less interest to him than their meaning. If Jesus is said to have cured blindness, it is a "sign" that he brings spiritual "illumination" (the symbolism is embedded in our language); if he feeds a multitude on an impossibly slender allowance of loaves and fishes, it is again a "sign" of the nourishment of the soul with the life of Christ himself. In this gospel the symbolism is integrated into a massive theology. But in the earlier gospels also it is present, though in a simpler—perhaps we

should say a more naïve—way. Whatever else may be
the value of the miracle stories, at least they are all
intended to affirm that where Jesus was, the presence
and power of God made itself felt. And this was so
from the beginning; it was remembered.

If anyone chooses to read the miracle stories of the
gospels as pictorial symbols of the power of spiritual
renewal which the first Christians found in their encounter with Jesus, without raising the question
whether it all happened just like that, he is not far
from the intention of John at least, and possibly of
the others. That the total impact of Jesus upon his
generation had this quality is a strongly attested fact,
and it has far-reaching significance.

But there is perhaps something more that might
be said about the credibility of these stories as (ostensibly) factual, though the question of their factual
accuracy has not the importance sometimes attached
to it. Are miracles "impossible"? It would probably
be wise to use the term with some caution. With the
flood of fresh discoveries about the behavior of matter, and of mind, we hardly know what is, and what
is not, possible. But whether or not they are impossible, it is said, at any rate "miracles don't happen."
Certainly they do not happen in ordinary circumstances. But the whole point of the gospels is that the
circumstances were far from ordinary. They were
incidental to a quite peculiar situation, unprecedented and unrepeatable. It was the inauguration of
a new set of relations between God and man. A
miracle in the sense of the New Testament is not so
much a breach of the laws of nature (a concept
which would have had little meaning for most people of the time), but rather a remarkable or exceptional occurrence which brought an undeniable sense
of the presence and power of God. It may be that if
we had been there we might have found a "scien-

tific" explanation of what the early Christians regarded as miraculous; and it is legitimate enough to
use such knowledge as we now have, for instance,
about the treatment of psychosomatic disorders, as
a help toward the explanation of some of the cures
reported in the gospels. But even so we should not
have explained just that element in the occurrences
which made them worth recording—the overwhelming impression of "the finger of God," in the vivid
phrase attributed to Jesus himself.

So much seemed worth saying, to meet the objection that the mere presence of miracle stories in the
gospels discredits them as historical records. Certainly they are primarily documents of the faith of
the earliest Christians; but it must be added that this
faith acted as a preservative of genuinely historical
memories without which it would never have arisen.
That these memories should include some unex-
plained features is in the nature of the case.

Assuming, then, that we have here narratives
which ask to be treated seriously, though not un-
critically, as a record of things that happened, we
may for a moment look more closely at their composition and structure. This may throw light on the
character of their contents. In spite of differences,
all four follow broadly a common pattern. The attentive reader cannot fail to be struck with the
amount of space allotted in them all to the closing
stages of the story: the arrest, trial, and execution of
Jesus, and the events immediately preceding and following. If the gospels were offered as "Lives of
Jesus," this allocation of space would be out of proportion. The intention of the writers is unmistakable: to lay all possible emphasis on these closing
scenes because of their intrinsic importance.

That they should have made an indelible impression on the memory of those who were involved in them, and on the imagination of those to whom the story was first told, we could well understand. But that is not all. From writings outside the gospels we know that in early Christian belief (to put it very broadly and without detail) the death and resurrection of Jesus Christ had the character of a decisive conflict in which the powers of evil did their worst and the sovereignty of God was conclusively asserted for the salvation of mankind. These events therefore were of more than merely historical interest; and yet it was important to affirm that the conflict did indeed take place on the field of history, and in relation to real problems arising out of human nature and society as they are. The problems are perennial; they took a particular form in the years when Pontius Pilate governed Judaea and Caiaphas was high priest in Jerusalem. Three of the most permanent factors in history were involved. Rome stood for political order, the priests and Pharisees for institutional religion, the Zealots for patriotism. All are good things, but we know only too well how they can become perverted, and how each of them can afford both stimulus and opportunity to the baser passions of mankind. Such was the situation that Jesus faced. The authors of the gospels would have us see how in that situation the cause of God was vindicated.

That is why they lay such stress on this part of their story; and not they alone, but the "original eyewitnesses and servants of the gospel" who transmitted the memories on which they worked. So much indeed we might gather from the brief summaries of the early preaching; and critical analysis of the gospels themselves leads us to believe that behind them lay at least three distinct and independent traditions about the closing events.[6] These must have been shaped in different environments and transmitted through different channels. It is therefore remarkable that, while they vary in detail as honest witnesses will vary in reporting matters which have touched them deeply, they follow the same thread of narrative. This must represent the story as it was told in the earliest days, when memories were still fresh. While the purpose of the authors in telling the story is clear, they have suggested its deeper meaning only by hints here and there. The tone is one of sober, unemotional realism, allowing the events to make their own impression by their inherent weight.

In these closing chapters the march of events is unbroken, as the narrative moves, with gathering intensity, toward the final catastrophe and recovery. The structure of the remaining parts of the gospels stands in strong contrast. There is little real continuity. What we find is a series of separate scenes—snapshots rather than a movie—and the four writers, who in the closing scenes were constrained to follow a fixed order of events, use a large liberty in arranging the separate stories they tell, and the arrangement comes out differently in each of them. As a rule, each scene forms a unit by itself, usually concise and stylized, driving home some particular point, with little attention to details which do not affect this point. A very large proportion of them make use of an incident, briefly sketched, to introduce a pregnant saying of Jesus. They are, in fact, a medium for conveying his teaching, just as much as are those sections of the gospels which are expressly devoted to a report of his sayings. It has been observed that where we have more than one version of a scene, the different versions generally agree rather closely in the report of what Jesus said, but use more freedom in telling the story which provides the occasion for it. A comparatively small number of these units of narrative can properly be described as "tales" about things that Jesus did, in which our authors spread themselves in picturesque or dramatic detail. And here again we note the same freedom of treatment, in contrast with the relative fixity of the report of the sayings. On occasion, details "wander" from one tale to another in the several gospels. We are led to suppose that the earliest tradition contained a wealth of reminiscences, informal, unorganized, but full of characteristic traits, and that out of these the stylized narratives were shaped, to serve the needs of preachers and teachers.

What emerges is a lively picture of the *kind* of thing that Jesus did, the *kind* of attitude which his actions revealed, the *kind* of relations in which he stood with various types of people he encountered, and the causes of friction between him and the religious leaders. The question, how far this or that story may be taken as an accurate account of what happened on this or that occasion is one upon which judgments will vary. Some, as they stand, may be found more credible than others. One or the other may be felt to be not in character. But taken together, these stories, told from many different points of view, converge to give a distinct impression of a real person in action upon a recognizable scene. When we add the wealth of sayings transmitted as such without any narrative setting, the total picture is enriched and given color and depth. It is upon this total picture that our reading of the personality and the career of the Founder of Christianity must be based.

III

PERSONAL TRAITS

I HAVE SAID THAT the reported sayings of Jesus bear the stamp of an individual mind. It may serve as a test of that statement if we now ask, How far is it possible to describe the characteristics of the mind that they reveal?

"The style is the man," they say. What, then, of the style of the teaching of Jesus as it has come down to us in the gospels? A large proportion of it comes in the form of short, crisp utterances, pungent, often allusive, even cryptic, laden with irony and paradox. This whole body of sayings, handed down through different channels of tradition, has an unmistakable stamp. It is impossible to suppose that they are merely the product of skillful condensation by early Christian teachers. They have the ring of originality. They betray a mind whose processes were swift and direct, hitting the nail on the head without waste of words.

There are longer passages with a marked rhythm of their own, which still makes itself felt after a double process of translation, from Aramaic into Greek and from Greek into English. Sometimes, indeed, it appears as if the Greek were only a thin disguise for an original which fell into the regular meters of Hebrew and Aramaic poetry. More often the rhythms are freer, but still with a marked balance and parallelism of clauses. Take, for example, such a passage as the following; it is given by Matthew and Luke with slight verbal differences, but the general structure is unmistakable:

Put away anxious thoughts
   about food and drink to keep you alive
     and clothes to cover your body.
Surely life is more than food,
   the body more than clothes.

Look at the birds of the air;
   they do not sow and reap and store in barns;
Yet your heavenly Father feeds them.

Consider how the lilies grow in the fields;
   they do not work, they do not spin:
And yet even Solomon in all his splendour
   was not attired like one of these.[1]

Here an imaginative apprehension of the wonder and beauty of nature, and of the unity of nature and man under the care of the Maker of both, has brought forth the appropriate literary form for its expression. We may recall other sayings which express this sense of wonder and even mystery in familiar natural phenomena. "A man scatters seed on the land; he goes to bed at night and gets up in the morning, and the seed sprouts and grows—*how, he does not know.*" [2] "The wind blows where it wills; you hear the sound of it, but *you do not know* where it comes from or where it is going." [3] Clearly we are in touch with a mind of a poetic and imaginative cast. This should never be forgotten in any attempt to understand the teaching of Jesus.

Further, whatever his theme, he thinks and speaks in concrete images and pictures in preference to general or abstract propositions. Thus, instead of saying "Charity should not be ostentatious," he says, "When you do some act of charity, do not announce it with a flourish of trumpets." [4] Where he might have said, "Personal relations are more important than religious observance," he makes a picture: "If, when you are bringing your gift to the altar, you suddenly remember that your brother has a grievance against you, leave your gift where it is before the altar. First go and make your peace with your brother, and only then come and offer your gift." [5] It is not accidental that both pictures have a suggestion of incongruity which is almost comic. Sometimes the picture is deliberately grotesque: "Why do you look at the speck of sawdust in your brother's eye, with never a thought for the great plank in your own?" [6]

It is this sense for the concrete, this delight in imaginative picture-making, that has shaped the "parables," which are so notable a feature of the gospels. The term "parable" covers a variety of literary forms, but all of them, as we meet them in the gospels, turn upon some familiar aspect of the human scene, depicted with economy of words and with unfailing realism. There are short stories: about a traveller who was robbed and lay wounded by the roadside until he was succored by a kindly stranger; about a capitalist who entrusted sums of money to his subordinates for investment, and what they did with it; about the employment of casual labor in a vineyard and the question of wages and hours that arose. There are rapid sketches of typical human

D

situations: fishermen picking over their catch, children quarrelling in the market place, a son watching his father at work and learning his craft by imitation. Sometimes a picture is conjured up by a simple turn of phrase: "When a lamp is lit, it is not put under the meal-tub"; "no one sews a patch of unshrunk cloth onto an old coat."

The "parables" (in the broad sense of the term) draw upon a wide range of accurate observation. Their Author is one who has noted with an interest, sympathetic but unsentimental, and sometimes humorous, that this is the way human beings behave. He has recognized their native virtues (the touching affection of a father for his scapegrace son, or the devotion of a shepherd to his flock), but also the odd mixture of human motives. There was a man who kindly got up at midnight to accommodate a neighbor in an emergency—but he did it because the fellow was making a nuisance of himself! A dishonest servant under notice of dismissal provided for his future by a business transaction which, to say the best of it, sailed near the wind. He was no doubt a scoundrel, but what an example to us all of resourceful action in a crisis!

In this last example it is impossible to miss the tone of irony, and this is something which is often present—more often than the casual reader might suppose. Sometimes it takes the form of the apparent reduction of great issues to the level of the banal. "When you are asked by someone to a wedding feast, do not sit down in the place of honor. It may be that some person more distinguished than yourself has been invited, and the host will come and say to you, 'Give this man your place.' Then you will look foolish as you begin to take the lowest place." 7 On the face of it, elementary advice on social behavior, with the most crudely prudential motive. Very likely some of the auditors took it as such. On further reflection it might dawn on them that there was more behind it. "Everyone who exalts himself will be humbled, and whoever humbles himself will be exalted"; the "moral" may have been attached by the writer of the gospel (it recurs in several places); but he has put the reader on the right track, though we should perhaps not be wrong in looking a little deeper still. It would be very much in the manner of Jesus to leave people to think out the implications for themselves. To take another example: "If someone sues you, come to terms with him while you are both on the way to court; otherwise he may hand you over to the judge, and the judge to the constable, and you may be put in jail." [8] Obvious horse sense—especially if you are not too sure about the administration of justice in your local court—but it was not just practical advice for litigants. No "moral" is appended, but in the light of the teaching of Jesus as a whole (to anticipate) it is not difficult to see that it touches upon one of its recurrent themes—that the people he addressed stood in a situation in which decision was urgent and delay dangerous. In the end it is concerned with the eternal issues of human destiny, but this is not on the surface. The assumption is that life is like that, from the lowest levels to the heights. The principles of human action, like the processes of nature, fall within a universal order established by the Creator, to be recognized at any level by those who have eyes to see and ears to hear. No circumstance of daily life is too trivial or commonplace to serve as a window into the realm of ultimate values, and no truth too profound to find its analogue in common experience.

Here then we have a whole range of imagery drawn from loving observation of nature and human life. There is, however, also a quite different range of imagery, where realism yields place to fantasy. Take for example the following passage:

> The sun will be darkened, the moon will not give her light; the stars will come falling from the sky, the celestial powers will be shaken. Then they will see the Son of Man coming in the clouds with great power and glory.[9]

Such images as these have a long history. They can be traced through many passages of poetry and prophecy in the Old Testament; they had a flourishing career in the "apocalypses" which pullulated in the period just before and just after the beginning of the Christian era; and they lived on. It is impossible to say how far such passages as that quoted above are authentic utterances of Jesus, and how far the imagery has seeped into the gospel tradition from the environment. The images employed were part of the mental furniture of the period; there is no reason why Jesus should not have employed them. There is in any case nothing original about them. Where we may look for originality is the way they are applied, and the meaning attached to them. For while this "apocalyptic" imagery was inherited, each writer was free to give it his own interpretation, and nothing is clearer than that the interpretation varies from one to another. We should certainly be prepared to find Jesus not less original than prophet or apocalyptist in his treatment of inherited material. So if he said, "You will see the Son of Man seated at the right hand of God and coming with the clouds of heaven," [10] or, "I watched how Satan fell, like lightning, out of the sky," [11] there is no reason to assume that he intended to describe supernatural phenomena which might, in any literal sense, be "seen"; nor is his meaning necessarily decided by the use of the imagery by other teachers—prior, contemporary, or subsequent. Of this more later.

This "apocalyptic" imagery, then, though it may be said to fall in with the "pictorial" manner of speaking to which he inclined, is not characteristic of Jesus. It was something which he shared with many others. What *is* characteristic and distinctive is the realism of the parables. This permits a further inference—and here we pass from the manner and style which are patent in the record to the personality behind them. The Author of the parables must have been genuinely interested in people; he must have enjoyed mixing with various types. As such the gospels represent him. He received and accepted invitations to festive occasions, more freely, his critics suggested, than a man of piety should. He dined with persons of respectable standing in local society, and he had at least one friend who moved in the highest ecclesiastical circles (he was "an acquaintance of the High Priest" [12]). But our informants draw special attention to his association with people who were neither socially accepted nor morally approved. He was censured as "a friend of tax-gatherers and sinners." [13]

The peculiar venom that clings to the term "tax-gatherer" has its source in the special situation. Under the Roman administration, indirect taxes (customs and excise) were collected by a method which lent itself to abuse. The right to collect was put up for sale and bought as a speculation (the Greek term properly means "tax-*buyer*"). The job was one that had to be done, and presumably it was possible to do it honestly, but the profession was one to attract the less scrupulous, and it had an unsavoury reputation; in Greek society "tax-gatherer" was a dirty word. In Jewish Palestine, to make things worse, the taxes were revenue for a detested foreign government, or for local rulers who were its puppets, and their collectors were to nationalist feeling no better than collaborators with the enemy, while for the ultra-pious Jew their close involvement with the "unclean" ways of Gentiles was in itself an offense. They were ostracized from decent society. This goes far to explain the astonishment and aversion which were aroused when Jesus associated with tax-gatherers. Obviously these dubious characters must have liked his company a good deal better than they would have liked that of his critics, even if these had not held them at arm's length.

It would be easy to misconstrue all this as indicative of no more than a sociable disposition. But this is certainly not the whole truth. When Jesus was criticized for the company he kept, he retorted, with caustic irony, "Healthy people don't need a doctor; sick people do." [14] They were patients and he the physician; and a main part of the treatment was just his friendship. He was drawn to those who were sick in mind or body, because they needed help that he could give.

Many stories in the gospels illustrate his sensitive response to such need, whether the trouble was physical or moral. By his sympathy and compassion, but also by the strength which they felt in him, he inspired his patients with a new confidence—with "faith," a term which in the gospels includes both trust in the goodness of God and the courage and firmness which derive from it. A father (we are told) came to Jesus in distress about the apparently incurable malady from which his young son was suffering: "If it is at all possible for you, take pity on us and help us." [15] Jesus replied, "If it is possible! Everything is possible to one who has faith." "I have faith," the father cried; "help my faithlessness." The superficial illogicality is illuminating. This was precisely what Jesus could do for people who were on the edge of despair. In this story there is something almost brusque about the way in which the man's appeal is answered. There is another story about a man who had given way to a chronic disability, and for years had nursed a grievance which excused him from doing anything about it ("Someone else always gets in before me!"). "Do you *want* to recover?" Jesus asked. "Then pick up your bed and walk." [16] Compassionate, certainly, but bracing too.

His sympathy was particularly marked with those who labored under a disabling sense of guilt. His assurance, "Your sins are forgiven," restored their self-respect and liberated moral energy. But it was not intended to suggest that the feeling of guilt was a morbid delusion, or that his patients were worrying themselves unnecessarily. To accept forgiveness meant both that they recognized a moral standard from which they had fallen, and that they intended to take to better ways. That Jesus did in fact inspire not only the intention but an effective redirection of effort is implicit in these stories. Among the many references to his friendship with the ill-reputed tax-gatherers there is one only which tells us something about the individual concerned—Zacchaeus, the wealthy inspector of taxes at Jericho, an enterprising little man who was perhaps no better and no worse than the average of his profession. It was thought shocking that Jesus should have accepted his hospitality. The outcome of the encounter is sufficiently indicated by what Zacchaeus is represented as saying: "If I have cheated anyone, I am ready to repay him four times over." "Salvation has come to this house today!" Jesus exclaimed.[17]

Again, it is recorded that on one occasion a group of lawyers brought before him a woman detected in adultery, with the hope that he would take the responsibility of pronouncing the ferocious sentence laid down in the Law of Moses (not enforced at that period), or alternatively, would by refusing to do so expose himself as one who condoned immorality. With characteristic irony he ostensibly corroborated the sentence of stoning, but gave it a twist: "That one of you who is faultless must throw the first stone." The group melted away. "Where are they?" he asked. "Did no one condemn you?" "No one, Sir," she answered. "No more do I condemn you. You may go. Do not sin again." [18] Compassion for the woman is no less marked than scorn for her accusers, but the final words have an astringency which rules out any suggestion of "permissiveness." If he said that "tax-gatherers and prostitutes" were more promising subjects than "scribes and Pharisees," it was in the sense that they were free from the odious complacency of the self-consciously pious. They were therefore more open to the physician's treatment.

All these stories (and there are many of them) make it clear that the persons concerned recognized an authority to which they yielded. When he said, "Your sins are forgiven," they actually believed him, which was sufficiently remarkable in the religious climate of the time, and results followed. It must have been the same sense of authority that led others to respond to astonishingly exacting demands. The accounts of the "calling" of disciples are bald, and less informative than we might wish, but it stands firm that Jesus called upon certain persons to cut loose from home, family and livelihood and commit themselves to an insecure and precarious existence—and all for the sake of a cause which they only dimly understood—and that they responded. What led them to do so we are not told; the reader is expected to understand that there was something personally compelling about him. Indeed, with all his ready sympathy and his tenderness toward those who needed help Jesus could evidently be a formidable person to encounter. Two incidents illustrate the public impact he made. In Galilee he faced a crowd of some thousands bent on revolt, and bent on making him lead it—obviously because they felt the presence of a natural leader—and induced them to disperse peaceably. In Jerusalem, he drove the traders from the outer court of the temple, apparently by sheer moral force. Both of these incidents we shall have to consider later. They are cited here for the light they throw upon the impression of authority which Jesus made on minds not naturally predisposed to sympathy with his aims.

The note of authority, we are told, was recognized in his public teaching. The tone of many of his sayings bears this out. His "I say unto you" ("I tell you," "Take my word for it.") is in all gospels an inseparable mark of his style. And not only did he pronounce decisively upon disputed points, but he was willing to pit his judgment against the venerable traditions of his nation, and even, it would appear, on occasion against provisions of the Law of Moses, divinely inspired as it was believed to be.

Yet the somewhat imperious tone of such sayings must be balanced by a consideration of another feature of the teaching not less prominent in our documents. The gospels report a number of dialogues in which Jesus is represented as arguing a point to a conclusion. They are usually summarized with the utmost brevity, but behind the concise and stylized form we can discern genuine discussions, in which, often enough, the questioner is led to answer his own question—to answer it as posed in a way he had not thought of before. Many of the parables, it is clear, were intended to serve this purpose: the auditor is invited to pass judgment upon a fictitious situation, and then challenged to apply the judgment to the actual situation.

Analysis of a well-known passage in the Gospel according to Luke will illustrate this. A lawyer asked the question, "What must I do to gain eternal life?" The ensuing dialogue runs somewhat after this fashion. Jesus: "What is your own reading of the Law?" The lawyer: "Love God and love your neighbor." Jesus: "You have your answer." The lawyer: "But who is my neighbor?" Then follows the familiar story of the "Good Samaritan" who befriended a stranger, and the question, "Which of the three proved neighbor to the man?" The lawyer: "The one who showed him kindness." Jesus: "Go and do as he did." [19] The conclusion is peremptory enough, but the questioner has been led to it by a process in which he has taken a real part. In such instances the authority of Jesus has been exercised in bringing people, against their will, it may be, to the point at which they had to face the responsibility of a decision. If a person declined the challenge, Jesus simply left it to him.

Mark tells the story of a well-to-do man who approached him for advice upon the same subject. He was a good young man, and Jesus, we are told, liked him. But he startled him with the challenge, "Sell everything you have and give to the poor, and come, follow me." The man could not face it. Jesus commented ruefully, "How hard it is to enter the kingdom of God! It is easier for a camel to go through the eye of a needle than for a rich man to enter the kingdom of God." [20] We must not miss the note of sympathy; he knew well what a lot he was asking; but he made the demand all the same. And yet when the man refused he made no attempt to bring persuasion or pressure to bear, but let him go away crestfallen. Authority was there, but an authority which respected the freedom of the person.

Authority it was, with no backing of official position or traditional prestige, to say nothing of legal sanctions or the ultimate sanction of force. It must have rested on some indefinable personal quality in Jesus himself. Our primary records hardly allow us to go further, except by inference. After his high-handed action in clearing the traders out of the temple court, we are told, Jesus was directly challenged with the question, "By what authority are you acting like this? Who gave you this authority?" He refused to answer except in evasive terms which suggested that if his questioners could not see for themselves it was useless to tell them.[21]

The nearest approach, perhaps, to a definition which Jesus countenanced was propounded by an army officer who wanted his help. The story is told by Matthew and Luke, with variations in detail but with close agreement in the essential points of the dialogue. The officer approached Jesus on behalf of a member of his family, or perhaps a favorite servant, who was seriously ill. In support of his plea he urged the following argument: "You need only say the word, and the boy will be cured. I know, for I am myself under orders, with soldiers under me. I say to one 'Go,' and he goes; to another 'Come here,' and he comes." [22] The implication is clear. He is himself responsible to his commanding officer, and he in turn to the local ruler, who in the end is subject to Caesar in Rome. And therefore the "company commander," just because he is loyally obedient to his superiors, can issue orders which have behind them the ultimate authority of the emperor himself. The authority which Jesus is expected to exert is subject to the same condition. It is a remarkable argument. At the least it suggests how the personality of Jesus impressed itself on a complete outsider. But still more remarkable is it that Jesus appears to have endorsed it, and this could be only in the sense that the authority he exercises is that of Almighty God, just because he is himself loyally obedient to him. This is put in explicit terms in the Gospel according to John: "I do nothing on my own authority, but in all I say I have been taught by my Father. He who sent me is present with me, and has not left me alone, for I always do what is acceptable to him. . . . The word you hear is not mine; it is the word of the Father who sent me." [23]

We note here a characteristic difference between John and the others. Matthew and Luke have allowed the truth about the authority of Jesus to come out obliquely; John puts it into the mouth of Jesus himself. In this he is employing a method not unfamiliar among Greek writers—historians and others —with whom he has some affinity. He gives what may appear to be revelations about the inner life of Jesus, in the words of Jesus himself, but they must often be read rather as John's interpretation, sometimes indeed expressed in theological language which would have been strange to the circles in which

Jesus actually moved. This is not to say that they should be disregarded in the attempt to understand the mind of Jesus. They are the product of a singularly penetrating intelligence which has long brooded over his remembered words and actions. In the instance we have just considered, as often, John is making explicit what must be read between the lines in the other gospels. But the reticence which they observe on such matters reflects, in all probability, a reserve which Jesus himself maintained, and which we must take to be characteristic of him.

A few well-attested sayings seem partly to break through the reserve. Certainly we cannot miss a pervading sense of dedication to a mission, which at times was a terrible burden: "I have come to set fire to the earth, and how I wish it were already kindled! I have a baptism to undergo, and how hampered I am until the ordeal is over!" [24] In spite of his readiness for all kinds of social contacts, his mission set him apart from other men. It is not surprising that there should have been moments when the sense of isolation in an unresponsive society became almost intolerable: "What an unbelieving and perverse generation! How long shall I be with you? How long must I endure you?" [25]

Yet at the heart of the storm there was a center of calm: "No one knows the Son but the Father; and no one knows the Father but the Son." [26] In the Gospel according to John this theme of the mutual "knowledge" of Father and Son is developed in theological terms; and indeed there is a whole theology implicit in it. But the saying as I have quoted it from Matthew (and Luke has it with slight verbal differences) is not theology but a spontaneous personal statement. It begins with a confession of the deep loneliness which was increasingly the lot of

Jesus; he has found no one who really knows or understands him, not even those nearest to him; but there is One who does know him—God, his Father. And in that same intimate, personal way he too knows God. Here, we may legitimately infer, is to be found the driving force and the source of energy for an almost impossible mission; here certainly the source of the inflexible resolution with which he went, knowingly, to death in the service of his mission. The words of the Fourth Gospel here ring true: "It is meat and drink for me to do the will of him who sent me until I have finished his work"; [27] and according to the same gospel he moved into the final loneliness of his friendless death with the words, as simple as they could well be, "I am not alone, because the Father is with me." [28] Upon what went on in his mind as the end approached one ray of light is permitted to fall: the prayer, "If it is possible, let this cup pass me by. Yet not as I will, but as thou wilt." [29] It is the final act of dedication to his mission, and the key to the whole of it.

IV

THE TEACHER

In the jewish society of his time Jesus found his place, to begin with, as a teacher of religion and morals. He was addressed as "Rabbi" (Master), and not only by his immediate followers, but also by strangers, including some who would themselves have claimed the same title. It is true that the title had not yet become (as it did by the end of the century) something rather like the equivalent of a university degree, conferring license to teach, but even as a courtesy title it implied public, if informal, acceptance as a teacher. It was as such that Jesus was at first regarded. It was as such that he attached "disciples"—the word used was a technical term for those who attended upon a rabbi and formed his "school." What did Jesus teach?

It is clear that there was a wide ground which he shared with other rabbis of his time. He accepted, as they did, the Old Testament as containing a divine revelation. He could assume its teaching as something well known to his audience: God is one; he is "Lord of heaven and earth"; [1] he is supremely good ("No one is good except God alone." [2]), and supremely powerful ("To God everything is possible." [3]). Because he is both good and powerful, he is to be trusted. Because he is Lord and King, he is to be obeyed. He is stern in judgment, but also "plenteous in mercy," as the Old Testament constantly declares. So far there is nothing which would be unfamiliar or unacceptable to any well taught Jew of the time. Similarly, in his ethical teaching he started on common ground. He could assume all that was best in the Old Testament, and in the teaching of contemporary rabbis. He offered interpretations of the Law of Moses as other rabbis did, as well as some criticisms of it on which they would not have ventured. Jewish scholars have shown that there is a considerable amount of rabbinic teaching which is markedly similar to that of Jesus in the gospels, which after all is what we should have expected. Indeed, we must suppose that a good deal of the current ethics of Judaism is silently taken for granted.

And yet, the teaching is oriented in a direction which differentiates it from rabbinic Judaism; the angle at which it touches life is different. This can perhaps best be appreciated if we start again with the parables, which, as we have seen, are the most characteristic part of the record of the teaching of Jesus. If we survey the whole body of parables we cannot but observe that a large proportion of them have a common theme, which we might describe as the arrival of "zero hour," the climax of a process, bringing a crisis in which decisive action is called for. A farmer has patiently watched the growth of his crop: "first the blade, then the ear, then full grown corn in the ear." [4] For the moment there is nothing he can do about it; the forces of nature are in charge. "But as soon as the crop is ripe, he plies the sickle, because harvest time has come," and if he lets the moment pass, the crop is lost. A trader in gems who is offered a pearl of outstanding value— the prize of a lifetime—must buy there and then, or someone else will get it, even if it means gambling his entire capital.[5] A defendant on his way to court had better settle in a hurry.[6] A servant under notice of dismissal must devise means of avoiding beggary without delay.[7] One picture after another drives home the same idea: a crisis calling for decision.

What was this "zero hour" he was speaking about? The gospels leave us in little doubt. It was the hour with which Jesus and his hearers were faced at the time of speaking. As harvest is the culminating point of the agricultural year, so this is the climax of centuries of growth. "Look round on the fields; they are already white, ripe for harvest. The reaper is drawing his pay and gathering a crop." [8] It is the time when the history of Israel, with all its unfulfilled promise, reaches fulfillment. "Happy the eyes that see what you are now seeing! I tell you, many prophets and kings wished to see what you now see, yet never saw it; to hear what you hear, yet never heard it." [9] More nearly explicit is a saying which Luke has rendered with almost telegraphic brevity: "Until John, it was the law and the prophets; since then, there is the good news of the kingdom of God." [10] That is to say, with the work of John the Baptist (who had recently been put to death) an old order was wound up, and a new order was inaugurated. It is characterized by "good news" about the "kingdom of God."

In Hebrew idiom this phrase means something more like "the reign of God," or even "the reigning of God," that is, God himself exercising his royal power. Jesus came into Galilee, says Mark, announcing this "good news," which the writer has formu-

E

lated in a kind of slogan: "The time has come; the kingdom of God is upon you!" [11] That meant, Here is God in all his power and majesty, confronting you where you live! What are you going to do about it? The Galilean public rightly divined that Jesus was here stepping outside the province of a rabbi. "He is a prophet," they said, "like one of the old prophets." [12]

Jesus did indeed stand in direct succession to the prophets of ancient Israel, whose message is preserved in the Old Testament. The prophets took their stand on the conviction that God has a hand in human affairs, and they therefore interpreted the events of their time with insight derived from their converse with the Eternal ("hearing the word of the Lord," as they expressed it). Similarly, we should understand Jesus' proclamation of the kingdom of God as an interpretation of the contemporary situation in terms of his knowledge of God. It was a significant situation on any showing. Within Judaism a crisis loomed which was bound to resolve itself one way or the other before long. In the wider world remarkable things were happening to the minds of men, and Jewish life could not be insulated from it. Things were happening; but *what* was happening? Then, as always, there were many possible secular answers to the question. What answer should be given by one who believed in God? The prophets had answered for their time in terms of "the counsel of the Most High." And so Jesus answered the question posed by the crisis he discerned in the words, "The time has come; the kingdom of God is upon you." This is "zero hour," the hour of decision. God was confronting men, more immediately, more urgently, than ever before, and an unprecedented opportunity lay before them.

The statement needs some examination. God, the

eternal, the omnipresent, can hardly be said to be nearer or farther off at *this* time than at *that*. If he is king at all, he is king always and everywhere. In that sense his kingdom does not *come;* it *is*. But human experience takes place within a framework of time and space. It has varying degrees of intensity. There are particular moments in the lives of men and in the history of mankind when what is permanently true (if largely unrecognized) becomes manifestly and effectively true. Such a moment in history is reflected in the gospels. The presence of God with men, a truth for all times and places, became an effective truth. It became such (we must conclude) because of the impact that Jesus made; because in his words and actions it was presented with exceptional clarity and operative with exceptional power. Jesus himself pointed to the effects of his work as signs of the coming of the kingdom: "If by the finger of God I drive out the devils, then be sure the kingdom of God has come upon you." [13] The saying is obviously figurative. To speak literally, God has no fingers, and there may or may not be such things as evil spirits; what the gospels call casting out devils we might describe, rightly or wrongly, in other terms. But the essential meaning is not obscure. In the presence of Jesus the dark forces within, which ravage the souls and bodies of men, were overcome and their victims made new. That it was so, is a fact so deeply imprinted on the records that it cannot reasonably be doubted. And this, Jesus said, was a sign that God was coming in his kingdom. It would not be accurate to say that Jesus brought in, or set up, the kingdom of God. That was the work of God himself, whose perpetual providence, active in every part of his creation, had brought about this significant moment, and the most significant feature in it was the appearance of Jesus himself. In his words and actions he made men aware of it and challenged them to respond. It was "good news" in the sense that it meant opportunity for a new start and an unprecedented enrichment of experience. But when a person (or a society) has been presented with such a challenge and declines it, he is not just where he was before. His position is the worse for the encounter. It is this that gives point to the tremendous warnings that Jesus is reported to have uttered about the consequences of rejection. That is why John, looking back on the career of Jesus as a complete episode, saw it as a day of judgment. "Now is the hour of judgment for this world," [14] he writes. "The light came into the world and men preferred darkness to light." [15] Light is a good thing; to encounter the reality which is God's presence in his world is in itself good. Whatever possibility of disaster may lurk within the choice which is offered, the facing of the choice, in the freedom which the Creator allows to his creatures, in itself raises life to greater intensity. The coming of the kingdom meant the open possibility of enhancement of life; it also meant the heightening of moral responsibility.

What response to the challenge did Jesus expect from his hearers? "The kingdom of God is upon you; repent!" So Mark's slogan runs. The word "repent" in English suggests being "sorry for your sins." That is not what the Greek word means. It means, quite simply, to think again, to have second thoughts, to change your mind. "Repentance," as the gospels mean it, is a readjustment of ideas and emotions, from which a new pattern of life and behavior will grow (as the "fruit of repentance").

The readjustment turns upon acceptance of "good news of God." The news was, in the first place, that

God was *here, now*. If once that was grasped, then everything that could be said about God had a new immediacy. What Jesus had to say about God, as we have seen, was expressed in language imaginative and emotive, which suggests rather than defines. We have noted how he dwelt upon the beauty and wonder of nature, and linked man with nature in one order where each level could be illuminated from another, and God was to be traced in all. At every level man meets his Creator, the Lord of heaven and earth, supreme in goodness and power, whose goodness is an exuberant generosity directed toward all his creatures without discrimination, and yet focussed on individuals in inconceivable intimacy. "Even the hairs on your head have all been counted." [16]

It is instructive to observe how this way of thinking about God gives a new color to images of Deity which Jesus took over from the tradition of his people. The idea of God as the Shepherd of Israel is almost a commonplace in the Old Testament. A true shepherd, Jesus observed, will be deeply concerned over a single sheep that has gone astray: "He goes after the missing one until he finds it." [17] So does God. And the point is sharpened because Jesus was censured for doing that very thing. The parable of the Lost Sheep, in fact (so Luke tells us), was his reply to such censures. The traditional image of the divine Shepherd was revivified in his actions as well as in his words.

Again, God as the Father of his people was a very familiar metaphor, deeply embedded in the religious language of Judaism. And indeed the idea of a Father-god is common to many religions. But what is fatherhood, in its essential meaning, as applied to the Deity? Jesus did not hesitate to compare it directly with ordinary human fatherhood. "If you, bad as you are, know how to give your children what is good for them, how much more will your heavenly Father give good things to those who ask him!" [18] The same comparison emerges in the parable which is perhaps the best known of them all, that of the Prodigal Son.[19] This is no ideal picture of an imaginary father, of such exceptional saintliness that he can stand for God himself. He is *any* father worth the name, as the hearers are expected to recognize, and this is how he would behave; and that is what God is like. Once again, the parable, we are told, was by way of a defense of what Jesus was doing against the censures of the pious, who are slyly satirized in the figure of the smug elder brother ("I never once disobeyed your orders!"). It is, in equal measure, an expression of the attitude of Jesus and an image of Deity.

All through, the teaching of Jesus about God is distinguished by the directness, warmth and simplicity with which the language of fatherhood is used. "You have a Father who knows that you need all these things." "It is not the will of your Father that one of these little ones should be lost." [20] The same qualities mark the prayer, used by the church from its earliest days, which was believed to have been taught by Jesus himself. The prayer as it is commonly used, now as for centuries past, in public worship agrees with Matthew's version of it, cast in a form which no doubt had such use in view. Luke gives a simpler, perhaps a more original version:

Father, thy name be hallowed.
Thy kingdom come.
Give us each day our daily bread.
And forgive us our sins,
    for we too forgive all who have done us wrong.
And do not bring us to the test.[21]

The word for "Father," which the earliest Christians
learnt from Jesus in their native Aramaic, was
"*Abba*" (the Aramaic word is preserved in some
places of the New Testament), and "*Abba*" was the
intimate mode of address from child to father in
the Jewish family. "My Father," or "our Father,"
was felt to be slightly more distant or more respect-
ful, and Matthew's "our Father in heaven" represents the formal language of liturgical prayer. Here
again is a slight but not insignificant pointer to the
way in which Jesus wanted his followers to think of
God. The actual petitions of the prayer agree with
this. They are the appeal of children to a father,
simple, direct and confident.

This kind of language, they say, is "anthropomorphic." Of course it is; and of course all human
language about God falls short of telling what he is
—the language of philosophical abstraction no less
than the poetic image. But it is nevertheless intended
to be taken seriously. In the first century many devout Jews were shy of such language. We can see
this from the way in which they paraphrased passages
in the Old Testament which sounded anthropomorphic, and from the circumspect terms in which
they spoke of the Deity ("Heaven," "The Name,"
"The Holy One, blessed be he," and the like). Some
of them, especially if they had come under Greek
influence, as had many Jews of that period, spoke of
"the One who really is," much as some moderns
speak of "the ultimate reality," or "the ground of
being." In contrast, the gospels are uninhibited in
their use of anthropomorphic language. We must
suppose that Jesus used it, by choice, because it is
the appropriate way of speaking about the personal
life with God which was his concern, but, even more,
because it was the only possible way of speaking of

God as he himself knew him. He was aware that there were sophisticated types who could not take his teaching; he accepted this as a part of the conditions under which he had to work. "I thank thee, Father," he is recorded to have said, in one of the very few echoes of his personal prayers that have come through into the gospels—"I thank thee, Father, Lord of heaven and earth, for hiding these things from the learned and wise, and revealing them to the simple." [22] Some people would need to make a considerable effort to put themselves into the attitude in which his teaching would have meaning for them. "Unless you turn round and become like children, you will never enter the kingdom of God"; or, in other words, "Whoever does not accept the kingdom of God like a child will never enter it." [23] This "turning round" is a large part of what is meant by "repentance" in the gospels. It is learning to think of God as your Father and of yourself as his child, quite simply.

How it would work out in daily practice is a question, it would seem, which Jesus was willing to leave very much to the awakened conscience of the individual. To bring about that awakening of conscience was a major object of his work, certainly the major aim of most of the parables. We look in vain in the gospels for any such elaborate scheme of rules for living as were offered by contemporary moralists, Jewish and Greek. This is not to be taken as meaning that there was either any vagueness about the true nature of moral action or any relaxation of the moral imperative. The follower of Jesus is under orders, no less binding because they are not spelled out in detail; he is "the man who hears these words of mine and acts upon them." [24] It is not because he wanted to let people off lightly that Jesus did not

dictate a set of bylaws. And in fact the gospels do
contain a small but illuminating body of directly
ethical instruction. To this we must now turn.

To start from a point where Jesus occupied common ground with his Jewish contemporaries may
help us to appreciate both the organic relationship
of his teaching to its matrix in Judaism, and the new
departure it marks. In the first century, some of the
most advanced of Jewish teachers, faced with the
growing complexity of the system of ethics contained
in the so-called Law of Moses and its constantly pro-
liferating interpretations and supplements, were attempting to bring out its central or overruling intention by giving prominence to one or another "great
commandment" upon which the rest might be supposed to hang. Jesus was aware of these attempts, and
in sympathy with them. It is recorded that in dis-
cussing the question he found himself in friendly
agreement with some teachers of the Law that there
are two "great commandments": Love God with all
your heart; love your neighbor as yourself. According to Matthew and Mark the combination of these
two commandments was suggested by Jesus, and his
questioner cordially agreed. According to Luke it was
the "lawyer" (as he calls him) who made the combination, and Jesus assented.[25] There is no reason
why both reports should not be true. It is likely
enough that the question was discussed on more than
one occasion.

Love of God; love of neighbor: an important part
of the ethical teaching of Jesus can be brought under
these twin heads, and this has often been done by
Christian moralists. But if we are to trust the three
earlier gospels, this was not his way. The objection
has often been raised, that love cannot be commanded, and that to say "Thou shalt love" involves

a contradiction. The objection may be rebutted in various ways. But in fact Jesus dealt with the theme to which the two commandments refer in a different way, which is not open to any such objection. Singular as it may appear, he seems to have said little (in express terms) about the duty of loving God, and not much more (in express terms) about loving one's neighbor, except where he was relating himself to current teaching with which his hearers would be familiar. Indeed he seems to have been sparing in his use of the word "love" (noun or verb).

Thus, when he is speaking in language of his own choice he does not say, "Thou shalt love God." He says (in effect) "God is your Father; become what you are, his child." To live as a child of God means, as a matter of course, trust and obedience. All that is in the Old Testament, and what Jesus says about it is only a re-emphasis. But there is a further point: the maxim "Like father, like child" holds good here, and it is in the application of this principle that we can recognize an emphasis which is characteristic of the teaching of Jesus. The child of God will be like his Father, at least to the extent that he will feel himself obliged to try to reproduce in his own behavior towards others the *quality* of God's action toward his children, and to pursue the *direction* in which that action points.

The "imitation of God" was a not uncommon way of expressing the moral ideal; it is found in both Jewish and Greek moralists of the period. They differ among themselves in regard to the divine attributes held up for imitation. For example, there were teachers for whom the characteristic attribute of Deity was the blissful serenity of perfectly self-centered indifference, and it was this that the "philosopher" must imitate. For others it was a transcen-

dent and ineffable "holiness," unrelated to the
conditions and values of human life on earth, to be
imitated in seclusion from the world, by a contrived
and exacting discipline. This appears to have been
the view of some Jewish sectaries. But in the best
Jewish teaching (going back to the prophets of the
Old Testament) the attributes of God which are to be
imitated are those which can be conceived on the
analogy of human virtues at their highest; such as his
even-handed justice, his mercy, his "faithfulness."
Jesus agreed: "Justice, mercy, and good faith" he
declared to be "the weightier demands of the
Law." [26] But he also put the subject in a fresh light
by his emphasis on the undiscriminating generosity
and sympathy of the heavenly Father, particularly
as shown towards those who are unworthy of it.
This is the divine quality, above all, in which children of God will be like their Father. He "makes
the sun rise on good and bad alike, and sends rain on
the honest and the dishonest." [27] This is not, in any
workaday sense of the term, justice: it is "goodness
beyond justice." And this is the kind of thing his
children should be doing. Whether this should be
called love to God or love to neighbor is a matter of
indifference. To love God is to live as his child; to
live as a child of God is to treat your neighbor as
God treats you.

But since the goodness of God is undiscriminating,
"beyond justice," the term "neighbor" is no longer
serviceable unless it is redefined. In the parable of
the Good Samaritan, where love to neighbor is, quite
simply, doing for him what needs to be done in
the emergency, the good neighbor is both alien and
heretic.[28] And at this point, perhaps, some hearers
who had assented so far might have had misgivings,
even if they did not go to the lengths of those

fanatical sectaries whose *Manual of Discipline* (found among the "Dead Sea Scrolls") enjoined them "to love all the children of light . . . and to hate all the children of darkness, each according to the measure of his guilt." It may have been with teaching of this kind in view that Jesus said, "You have learned that they were told, 'Love your neighbor and hate your enemy.' But what I tell you is this: Love your enemies." He was at pains to dot the i's and cross the t's of this challenging revision of the old commandment, "Love your neighbor."

> If you love only those who love you,
>   What credit is that to you?
>   Even sinners love those who love them.
> If you do good only to those who do good to you,
>   What credit is that to you?
>   Even sinners do as much.
> And if you lend only where you expect to be re-
>   paid,
>   What credit is that to you?
>   Even sinners lend to sinners, to be repaid in
>   full.
> But you must love your enemies and do good,
>   And lend without expecting any return;
> And you will have a rich reward:
>   You will be sons of the Most High,
>   Because he is kind to the ungrateful and the
>   wicked.[29]

It is impossible to miss the stress laid upon breaking out of the narrow circle within which it is natural to confine the love of neighbor, and this is specifically related to the quality of the divine action. It is also instructive to observe how the expression slides from "Love your enemy," modelled on the traditional "Love your neighbor," to "Do good," "Lend," becoming more concrete at each step. At a still further stage the expression becomes fully pictorial and we get what is in effect a parable. "If someone slaps you on the right cheek, turn and offer him your left. If a man wants to sue you for your shirt, let him have your coat as well. If a man in authority makes you go one mile, go with him two." (The reference is to the system of forced labor for the state which was employed under the Roman Empire, especially for the purposes of the imperial postal service.) "Give when you are asked to give, and do not turn your back on a man who wants to borrow." [30] Considered as regulations for the conduct of daily life these maxims are utopian. They were not intended as such regulations. Yet they are meant to be taken seriously. They are vivid and even startling illustrations, in extreme cases, of the way in which the quality and direction of God's treatment of his children might be reproduced in human relations. The very extravagance of them shows that Jesus was well aware what a lot he was demanding of human nature when he substituted "Love your enemies" for "Love your neighbor." There is a somewhat similar note of extravagance in an illuminating little dialogue reported by Matthew. Jesus has been urging the duty of forgiveness. Peter is represented as asking, "How often am I to go on forgiving my brother if he goes on wronging me? As many as seven times?" Jesus replies, "I do not say seven times; I say seventy times seven." [31] Four hundred and ninety times— which is absurd. Peter's question is one which would occur' naturally enough to a well-brought-up Jew of the period. He had been taught that forgiveness was a virtue, and, in the spirit of much contemporary exposition of the Law, he would like to know exactly how far he was expected to go. The reply of Jesus is a *reductio ad absurdum* of any quantitative treatment of the question. There are no limits.

It might be asked why Jesus gave such prominence to these themes. One answer might be that he saw, as any sensitive observer might have seen, that Jewish society was being corroded by rancorous hatreds, among the parties and factions into which it was divided, and between Jew and Roman. It was the part of any publicist who had insight and foresight, to point this out and to urge a change of temper before it was too late. But there is more to it than that. It is in this field of human relations, where the issues are most acute and the emotions are most strongly aroused, that the absoluteness of God's requirements can be exposed. This is a part of what is meant by the declaration that his kingdom is here. It is no time for the nicely calculated less and more of "practical" morality. It is a time for total commitment. There is no limit to what is demanded of children of God, nor can his demands be exhaustively fulfilled. "When you have carried out all your orders, you should say, 'We are servants and deserve no credit; we have only done our duty.' " [32] All that a man can do is to accept full responsibility before God, and to throw himself on his mercy. Forgiveness to "seventy times seven" is a function of the heavenly Father. But "if you do not forgive others, then the wrongs you have done will not be forgiven by your Father." [33] This is not to be taken as a threat of retributive action on the part of God. It means that the unforgiving person does not stand in the relation of a child to the heavenly Father. He has broken that relation by his own attitude; he has placed himself outside the family of God. "Observe," Paul once wrote, "the kindness and the severity of God." [34] We can observe both here, in a tension which must not be evaded, if the teaching of Jesus is to be understood. A similar combination of kindness and severity is to be observed in his own attitude. His tenderness to men in their need, and his unsparing demands upon them, both arise from a deep concern for the individual as a child of the heavenly Father, and this reflects the attitude of God himself, as Jesus represented it.

We have seen that Jesus started from positions which he largely shared with other Jewish teachers of his time, but that in some respects he went beyond these positions. It is clear that a rift soon appeared, and this became with time an irreconcilable breach. In interpreting what the gospels report upon this subject it is well to bear in mind that, when they came to be written, controversy between the followers of Jesus and official Judaism had gone forward with increasing bitterness for some years before the final separation of church and synagogue. It was almost in-evitable that in the course of this controversy the sayings of Jesus should sometimes have been given a sharper edge, certainly that those sayings should be most often repeated which were capable of such a sharp edge. But that he did upon occasion set his teaching in deliberate opposition to that of other rabbis cannot be doubted. Nor, whatever allowance be made for overcoloring in the course of controversy, is it possible to doubt that he did deliberately criti-cize them, and sometimes in trenchant terms, though we need not assume that *all* of them were included in such criticism; there were perhaps more teachers of the Law with whom Jesus could find himself in friendly agreement than the two or three who have found their way into the gospels. But a growing op-position is a feature of the record which cannot be set aside. In any study of the beginnings of Christianity it is necessary to take account of this opposition and to try to understand its nature and causes. Moreover, in the attempt we may hope to arrive at a juster appreciation of the distinctive tendencies and emphases of the teaching of Jesus himself.

It is evident from what has already been said that the ethics of Jesus are predominantly concerned with the dignity and responsibility of the human individual face to face with God. In view of this it is not surprising to find a certain impatience with minutiae of religious etiquette with which the most influential school of rabbinic Judaism was much preoccupied. Not that he seems to have set himself deliberately to undermine the cherished customs of his people. A good example is his treatment of the law of tithe, a tax of 10 per cent for religious purposes levied on agricultural produce. It laid a serious burden on those who tried to observe it with scrupulous exactness, for it was, of course, in addition to the imperial taxation. It was no bad test of genuine devotion to the Law. Upon this there is a saying of Jesus, reported (with small verbal differences) by Matthew and Luke: "You pay tithes of mint and dill and cummin, but you have overlooked the weightier demands of the Law—justice, mercy and good faith. It is these you should have practiced, without neglecting the others. Blind guides! You strain off a midge, yet gulp down a camel!" [35] Jesus was not intolerant of these religious practices; there is no harm in having rules of discipline, and if such rules are accepted, certainly no harm in following them conscientiously. But there is a proportion to be kept; if they are allowed to get in the way of those personal relations which are summed up as "justice, mercy and good faith," then the attempt to keep the Law of God is frustrated.

It was on similar grounds that Jesus sat loose to other current rules of discipline; for example, the regulations about sabbath observance, which had become immensely elaborate and detailed. Here again it does not appear that he planned to undermine the conventions of Jewish society. We are told that he was accustomed to attend the synagogue service on the sabbath, and we may assume that normally he would conform with the rules generally observed. But when these rules conflicted with elementary human need, they must give way. In principle, indeed, this was conceded. "The sabbath was given to you, and not you to the sabbath": the sentiment is attributed to more than one Jewish rabbi. Jesus agreed: "The sabbath was made for the sake of man, and not man for the sabbath." [36] But his actions implied a more thorough application of it than others were prepared to allow. He gave serious offense by treating patients, not in immediate danger of death, on the holy day. When challenged, he propounded the question, "Is it permitted to do good on the sabbath, or to do evil?" If the rules prevent you from doing good, that is, from promoting the welfare of any individual person who may be within your reach (your "neighbor"), then the rules must yield to a higher claim. There may also be a hint that to fail to "do good" because it is the sabbath is to "do evil."

The keeping of the sabbath may seem to us a comparatively trivial issue, but it was a sensitive point. It was one of the most obviously distinctive of all Jewish customs; it was one which the Gentile observer, however superficial, could not miss, as references in Greek and Roman literature sufficiently

F

prove. Nor was it forgotten that in the first great national revolt, two hundred years earlier, Jewish fugitives had allowed themselves to be massacred rather than fight on the holy day. The sabbath was specially prized as a mark of the separateness of the chosen people, and to attack it was to blur the national image.

Without going into further detail, we can see how inevitable it was that tension arose between Jesus and the exponents of current religious practice. But the trouble went deeper than the lack of proportion and sheer triviality to which their casuistry sometimes descended. Jesus saw in it the grave danger of such an emphasis on the overt act that the inner disposition was forgotten. He is reported to have put the point by way of an interpretation of two of the Ten Commandments. "You have learned that our forefathers were told, 'Do not commit murder; anyone who commits murder must be brought to judgment.' But what I tell you is this: anyone who nurses anger against his brother must be brought to judgment." And again, "You have learned that they were told 'Do not commit adultery.' But what I tell you is this: if a man looks on a woman with a lustful eye he has already committed adultery with her in his heart." [37]

There is nothing here that need have upset anyone who was acquainted with the Old Testament or with Jewish teaching of the time. There are many rabbinic sayings which condemn the indulgence of anger (against a fellow Jew, *bien entendu*), and the Ten Commandments themselves not only prohibit adultery but add, "Thou shall not *covet* thy neighbor's wife." But this constant and emphatic dwelling on the inward disposition rather than the overt act might well excite the suspicion of those who insisted on the

deed as the sole visible test of obedience to the
Law of God. It is clear that Jesus too attached importance to the concrete act; that is one reason why he
cast so much of his ethical teaching in the form of
vivid word pictures of action instead of abstract general maxims. But he did so with the proviso that
the act is the sincere expression of an inward disposition. "A good man produces good from the store
of good within himself, and an evil man from the
evil within produces evil. For the words the mouth
utters come from the overflowing of the heart." [38] It
is a matter of wholeness of character, consistency of
thought, word and act.

That is why he expressed such horror of ostentatious display of religion where a true inward devotion was lacking. "Be careful," he is reported to
have said, "not to make a show of your religion before men. . . . When you pray, do not be like the
hypocrites; they love to say their prayers standing up
in synagogues or at the street corners, for everyone to
see them. . . . When you pray, go into a room by
yourself, shut the door, and pray to your Father who
is there in the secret place." [39] When he was censured
for laxity in observing the traditional rules about
ceremonial washing before meals, he retorted upon
his critics in a biting phrase: "You clean the outside
of cup and plate, but inside you there is nothing
but greed and wickedness." [40] Again, it was held that
certain kinds of food "defile" the eater. According to
Mark Jesus pronounced categorically on the matter:
"Nothing that goes into a man from outside can
defile him." Mark adds an explanation: "From the
inside, out of a man's heart, come evil thoughts [and
a whole catalogue of violent and criminal practices].
These evil things come from inside, and they defile
the man"; and he adds, as his own comment, "thus

he declared all foods clean." The distinction between "clean" and "unclean" foods was deeply embedded in the Jewish system and had its basis in the
Old Testament itself. It has been doubted whether
Jesus can have gone so far, but there seems no reason
to question Mark's report of the basic saying. It was
known to Paul, who wrote, several years before
Mark's gospel appeared: "I am absolutely convinced,
on the authority of the Lord Jesus, that nothing is
impure in itself." [41] If he did say something to this
effect, it is no wonder hostility was aroused. In times
of persecution, the test of loyalty to the Jewish religion had often been just this refusal of "unclean"
food. Was it possible to repudiate a principle which
the martyrs had sealed with their blood?

Contemporary rabbis would not have dreamed of
denying the importance of inward disposition. But
Jesus pressed the principle with such ruthless logic
that it seemed in danger of eroding the discipline by
which social morals were safeguarded. For him it was
a point of cardinal significance: an act is a moral
act only so far as it expresses the whole character of
the man who acts. His severest strictures are directed
against those teachers of religion and morals whose
lofty principles were belied by the pretentiousness,
superficiality and inhumanity of their behavior.
The strictures are severe enough; it is possible, as
we have seen, that our reports of them have been
colored by subsequent controversy. But that they
were not without grounds we may learn from passages
in the rabbinic writings themselves which castigate
unworthy claimants to the honored name of
"Pharisee" in terms no less scathing than those of
the gospels. But all this is in a sense a side issue,
significant only insofar as it illustrates the moral
bias of the teaching of Jesus as a whole. And this

bias can equally be felt in his strictures on followers
of his own in whom he detected the same lack of
moral consistency. "Why do you keep calling me
'Lord, Lord'—and never do what I tell you?" [42] So
runs a characteristically pointed saying in Luke. In
Matthew it is enforced by a telling piece of imagery,
in which Jesus imagines himself confronting these
unworthy followers on a day of judgment beyond this
world. "When that day comes, many will say to me,
'Lord, Lord, did we not prophesy in your name, cast
out devils in your name, and in your name perform
many miracles?' Then I will tell them to their faces,
'I never knew you; out of my sight, you and your
wicked ways!' " It was not only Pharisees who had to
feel the lash of his tongue.

But the fact is that his whole approach to morals
was different from that which prevailed among
Jewish teachers of his time. The formidable structure of tradition with which the Law of Moses had
come to be surrounded was designed to bring its
demands within the compass of the individual by
making every command applicable in a clearly defined way to each situation in which he might find
himself. He must know, for example, just how far
he might walk on a sabbath day without infringing
the commandment, and exactly what circumstances
might justify him in stretching it. (It was to the
credit of the Pharisees that they did stretch it—for
example, to save life—but within strict limits.)
Something of the kind, no doubt, is necessary if
ethics are to be made practicable; we can hardly
dispense with casuistry. But it has its dangers. Beside the obvious danger of giving the outward act
an independent value apart from the disposition
which makes it a moral act, there is a more subtle
danger, that of a quantitative conception of moral-

ity. It is as if there were a set of regulations each of which, like the questions in an examination paper, earned a certain number of marks, and the total could be put to a man's credit. The implication would be that it is possible to score full marks, and to say with a good conscience (as someone says in the gospels), "I have kept *all* these." [43] Jesus had severe things to say about "those who were sure of their own goodness and *looked down on everyone else*." [44] That, of course, is the trouble. The yardstick by which one measures one's own (real or supposed) excellence also measures the other man's defects, to one's own great comfort. In the teaching of Jesus, goodness is not measurable by any yardstick. It is qualitative and not quantitative at all. It is the effort to reproduce the *quality* of the divine action. The effort may be present at lowly levels of achievement; the quality itself is never fully present at the highest, since "no one is good [in the absolute sense] except God alone." There is therefore no ground either for complacency or harsh judgment on the part of the "virtuous," or for self-despair on the part of the "sinner." It is surprising how often the sayings of Jesus recur to this theme, of the folly and evil of self-righteousness and censoriousness. His heaviest count against the prevailing teaching of his time is precisely this: that, starting with the best intentions, it had come to encourage this folly and evil, as if it were inseparable from a high moral standard.

It is clear that there breathes through all this a lively sympathy with those whose weakness, or whose lack of opportunity, placed them at a disadvantage. But it would be misleading to regard it as nothing more than the protest of a warm-hearted, liberal-minded humanitarian. It arose out of the conviction that with the coming of the kingdom of God a new era in relations between God and man had set in. Morality might now draw directly from fresh springs. The whole apparatus of traditional regulations lost its importance. Jesus never intended a campaign against the Law. It might still serve a useful purpose in its way; it might be understood as bearing witness to the two "great commandments." But it was no longer central, and no longer constituted the whole structure of moral obligation.

The differences, therefore, which produced first a rift and then an irreconcilable opposition between Jesus and the dominant school of Jewish teachers in his time were not in the end (though they might appear at first sight to be) a matter of divergent interpretations of this or that point in the Law. After all, there was considerable latitude of interpretation among accredited rabbis—more latitude at that period than in the reformed Judaism which emerged after the debacle of A.D. 70. But his critics rightly divined that his teaching threatened the integrity of Judaism as a system in which religion and national solidarity were inseparable.

This was the secret of the fatal breach, as it is pinpointed by a modern Jewish writer, and one who is by no means insensitive to the many noble ideas which he finds in the teaching of Jesus.[45] He writes:

The Judaism of that time, however, had no other aim than to save the tiny nation, the guardian of great ideals, from sinking into the broad sea of heathen culture and enable it, slowly and gradually, to realize the moral teaching of the Prophets in civil life and in the present world of the Jewish state and nation. Hence the nation as a whole could only see in such public ideals as those of Jesus an abnormal and dangerous phantasy; the

majority, who followed the Scribes and Pharisees
(The *Tannaim*), the leaders of the popular party,
could on no account accept Jesus' teaching. This
teaching Jesus had absorbed from the breast of
Prophetic, and, to a certain extent, Pharisaic Judaism; yet it became, on the one hand, the negation
of everything that had vitalized Judaism; and, on
the other hand, it brought Judaism to such an
extreme that it became, in a sense, non-Judaism.

This, a judgment from within the rabbinic tradition, may probably be accepted as being, up to a
point, a fair assessment of the grounds of the opposition which Jesus encountered from a party with
which in some respects he had much in common. If
this seems hardly sufficient to account for a hostility
which could be satisfied with nothing short of
his death, we may recall that the time was one in
which resentment of pagan domination was mounting
high, and hot passions were stirred in defense of the
cherished values of "the Jewish way of life." Yet
there is something about the antagonism, as it is reflected in the gospels, which seems to draw from an
even deeper spring than apprehension of a threat to
the national heritage. Jesus was charged with
"blasphemy." The term is a heavily loaded one, and
the charge suggests an affront to powerful sentiments
of religious reverence and awe, evoking both hatred
and fear. The charge of blasphemy expresses not so
much a rational judgment as a passionate, almost
instinctive, revulsion of feeling against what seems
to be a violation of sanctities. There must have
been something about the way in which Jesus spoke
and acted which provoked this kind of revulsion in
minds conditioned by background, training and
habit. It was this, over and above reasoned objections

to certain features of his teaching, that drove the Pharisees into an unnatural (and strictly temporary) alliance with the worldly hierarchy, whose motives for pursuing Jesus to death were quite other. But of this more later.

V

THE PEOPLE
OF GOD

Aɴʏ sᴛᴜᴅᴇɴᴛ ᴏғ ᴛʜᴇ Graeco-Roman world at the beginning of our era who tries to penetrate beneath the surface of the political, economic and military history of the period and discern what was going on in the minds of men, becomes aware of a widespread expectation of a turn for the better in human affairs, even the dawn of a golden age, after the violent convulsions which had disturbed society for a century or more. There was something of a religious faith about it. It invoked oracles and prophecies, ancient and modern. It was often associated with the figure of a "savior," or deliverer—a great man, perhaps a superman with something of divinity about him, if indeed he was not a god. Millions of the subjects of Rome saw the emperor himself as the divine deliverer. A Roman poet hailed Augustus as *praesens divus,* a "present deity." [1] The emperor disposed of powers which seemed nothing short of miraculous to the subject peoples of the eastern provinces, who had lived for two or three generations in a disintegrating society. He had given unity to a distracted world. He could guarantee peace, safety from outward attacks, and a measure of social security internally. At the least he could provide everybody with "bread and circuses." The emotion which expressed itself in the worship of the emperor as a very god on earth was genuine. He was the savior, the "restorer of the world" (*restitutor orbis*). It was not difficult for propagandists of the empire to represent it as trembling on the verge of a millennium. Under Augustus it really did seem to many as if a golden age might be round the corner. By the time of Tiberius (to whose reign the events of the gospel history belong), the gilt was tarnished.

The Jews were not greatly impressed by imperial claims of this sort. But they shared in the general hope of a good time coming. Certainly they had their quest for "present deity." In the distant past, they believed, the great God had revealed himself to Moses and the prophets; he had acted in the deliverance of Israel from Egypt and the restoration after the Babylonian conquest. There was a deep longing that at this time of need, when Israel was again oppressed, he should once again manifest himself in appropriate action, and there was a varying degree of confidence that he would do so.

As the secular hope of a golden age had its prophecies and oracles, so the Judaism of this period produced that curious literature known as "apocalyptic." It professed to unveil the future—the near future—in visions, usually fantastic enough, and always in the sense of some glorious destiny impending for the chosen race. Inevitably, among large sections of the population the picture took on colors similar to those of the secular golden age. The place of the divine emperor, victorious in war, beneficent in peace, was taken by the ideal figure of the "Son of David," a wise and powerful king of the old legiti-

mate line. He would be the Caesar of a Jewish empire no less universal than the Roman; though it
would be fair to say that the program drawn up for
the "Son of David" in literature not far in date from
the time of Jesus has more about justice and moral
reformation than about bread and circuses. To this
ideal figure was often given the title "Messiah." The
term was suggestive rather than precise in meaning.
In itself it meant no more than a person "anointed,"
or consecrated, to an office of special solemnity; but
always it was an office bound up with the peculiar
status of Israel as God's own people. In historical
retrospect, David, the idealized founder of the
Israelite monarchy, was "the Lord's Anointed"
(Messiah), *par excellence,* and the coming deliverer
was to be in some sort a second David. Such seems
to have been the most popular form of the "messianic" idea. *Vis-à-vis* Rome it spelt rebellion, and
many were ready to implement it in that sense.

This militant "messianism," however, was not the
only form taken by the national hope. The ancient
synagogue prayer, "Bring back our judges as at the
first, and our rulers as aforetime, and be thou king
over us, O Lord, thou alone," combined the sober
plea of a subject people for the recovery of independence with a genuinely religious aspiration. God
was the rightful King of Israel; every Jew was taught
that; but the effective reign of God was something
hoped for rather than experienced. And so again the
prayer was offered in the synagogue liturgy: "May
he establish his kingdom in your lifetime and in your
days, and in the lifetime of the whole house of
Israel." What the establishment of the "kingdom of
God" might in practice mean was something about
which minds might differ because of their different
background, education and discernment. According

to such differences various schools and parties had their several programs. But behind all the programs there remained the august idea of God himself coming to reign as sovereign, the living God, present and powerful, a factor to be reckoned with. This idea was waiting to be revived.

Then Jesus came into Galilee proclaiming, "The time has come; the kingdom of God is upon you!" It is not surprising that some understood him to be speaking of the kingdom of the Son of David with its revolutionary implications. The misunderstanding dogged his mission to the end, until he was put to death by the Romans as "king of the Jews." A misunderstanding it was, and one of fatal consequence. Yet a misunderstanding may be a truth distorted by a mere shift of level or perspective. So it was here. Jesus held aloof from all the party programs; he cut through them all to the root idea of "present deity"—God in all his power and majesty confronting individual men and women and demanding response; and to this idea he gave fresh clarity and strength, as we have seen. But it would be wrong to suppose that he so "spiritualized" the idea of the kingdom of God as to make it relevant only to the inner life of the individual. Aloof in one sense, he was nevertheless engaged with the contemporary life of his own nation. When he welcomed the "repentance" of an unpopular tax-collector, he spoke of him as a "son of Abraham." [2] When he defied censure to treat a crippled woman on the sabbath, she was a "daughter of Abraham." [3] The expressions are revealing. As individuals they were important to him, but they were also members of a people; their plight concerned the historic community to which they, and he, belonged, and their "salvation" (physical or moral) also concerned the well-being of

the community as a whole. Jesus spoke in parable
of the finding of lost sheep, and emphasized the
importance of the single sheep that went astray; but
it was to "the lost sheep of the house of Israel," [4] he
said, that he was sent. It is clear that in speaking of
the kingdom of God he was not less aware than any
contemporary Jewish teacher of the long tradition
that Israel is the people over which God is rightfully
king, in and through which his kingdom is to be
realized.

This tradition the prophets of the Old Testament
had made a part of the whole Jewish heritage of
thought. They insisted that God works in history,
and works through a community dedicated to his
purpose, a "people of God" or divine commonwealth.
Israel was intended to be such a people; that was its
raison d'être. Indeed that was the implication of
the name Israel itself as it was now used; it had
ceased to have either geographical or political significance after two Israelite monarchies had been
quashed some centuries earlier. Henceforward it
carried ideal overtones. The Jewish community had
been reorganized by the reformers of the fifth century
B.C. on the understanding that its whole corporate
life should be governed by the sacred law which was
believed to express the will of God. It was a brave
and honest attempt to create a society in which the
kingdom of God might be realized. But it had mis-
carried. The condition of Judaea in the first century
was pathological. It was torn with faction; a largely
secularized priesthood furthered its own ambitions
by subservience to the foreign power; the mass of
the people seethed with impotent hatred of Rome.
The efforts of good and devoted religious teachers
had the effect of widening the breach between the
pious and the despised "people of the land." The

situation worsened until it issued in the rising of A.D. 66, which brought the end of Jewry as a political entity.

Jesus was alive to the danger threatening his people. Neither they nor their leaders, he said, could "interpret the signs of the times," [5] and one has only to read the account of the period by the contemporary Jewish historian Josephus to see how true it was. As the ancient prophets had pointed to a threat from Assyria or Babylon, so in the time of Jesus the Roman peril loomed. On one occasion he was told of a clash in the temple, in which some Galileans had been slaughtered by the Roman soldiery. About the same time, as it happened, one of the towers on the wall of Jerusalem had fallen, with fatal results. His comment was: "Do you imagine that, because these Galileans suffered this fate, they must have been greater sinners than anyone else in Galilee? . . . Or the eighteen men who were killed when the tower fell on them at Siloam—do you imagine they were more guilty than all the other people living in Jerusalem? I tell you, they were not; but unless you repent, you will all of you come to the same end." [6]

"Unless you repent"; the call to "repentance" was addressed to individuals, certainly, but to individuals as members of a nation which was intended to be a "people of God" but had lost its way. If we ask what overt result Jesus may have hoped for, the answer is not easy, because he issued no program of religious or political reform, any more than he laid down precise regulations for individual behavior. He disclaimed any intention to reform the existing system. It would, he said, be no more sensible than patching a worn-out coat with new cloth. But it may be legitimate to ask, for example, what difference it might have made to the internal situation if those superior persons who "were sure of their own good-ness and looked down on everyone else" could have changed their minds, or if the orthodox Jew could have been persuaded to accept the Samaritan as a "neighbor"; what difference to external relations if the pious sectaries of Qumran, feeding their frus-trated animosities on fantasies of a holy war against Rome, could have learned that "love your neighbor" does not necessarily mean "hate your enemy," or if the entrenched hierarchy could have been persuaded to make the temple a home of real religion—and a desegregated home at that, "a house of prayer for all the nations." [7] Such questions are idle except as a help to the imagination, by way of making concrete, in an actual historical situation, the bearing of the principles that Jesus laid down. But he promulgated no program, nor does it appear that he ever con-templated attempting to take over the Jewish establishment as a going concern and reshape it to his mind (as, shall we say, the English reformers of the sixteenth century took over the ecclesiastical estab-lishment). It was not on that level that his mission proceeded.

The immediate prelude to his mission was that of John the Baptist, an enigmatic figure about whom we are told enough to stimulate conjecture, but too little to give much certain knowledge. A few sayings of his, however, preserved in the gospels, are un-questionably authentic. One of them runs as follows: "Do not presume to say to yourselves, 'We have Abraham for our father.' I tell you that God can make children for Abraham out of these stones here." [8] The implication is obvious: hereditary mem-bership of the chosen people is no passport to membership of the true people of God. To bring the

G

new "Israel" out of the existing system a fresh start must be made, and it must be by a creative act of God. That was John's view; it is unlikely that Jesus was less radical than he. Indeed only a like radicalism can explain some of his words and actions reported in the gospels.

In this, as in so much else, Jesus stood in succession to the Hebrew prophets, of whom, he said himself, John the Baptist was the last and greatest. Time and again, facing national calamities, the prophets repeat in varying imagery that the true people of God will emerge through his power from apparently final disaster. It will be like a resurrection of dead men's bones.[9] The calamities the nation suffered dramatized, as it were, the just judgment of Almighty God upon their evil courses; but within the judgment lay the mercy of God, with power to create anew; and that was why, beyond all hope, the nation revived. Thus far the prophets. Jesus declared that the supreme crisis was now here. His own generation was caught up in a drama of divine judgment which summed up all the judgments of the past. "This generation will have to answer for the blood of all the prophets shed since the foundation of the world."[10] That was how he saw the approaching catastrophe. It was no satisfaction to him to have to announce it. On his last ride to Jerusalem, when the ridge was surmounted and the city came in sight, he is said to have wept as he exclaimed:

> If only you had known, on this great day, the way that leads to peace! But no, it is hidden from your sight. For a time will come, when your enemies will set up siege works against you; they will encircle you and hem you in at every point; they will bring you to the ground, you and your children

within your walls, and not leave you one stone
standing on another, because you did not recognize God's moment when it came.[11]

It was in these realistic terms that Jesus saw the
plight of his nation. Yet the peril of a clash with
Rome only brought to the surface something deeper
than any political crisis. They were living through
a spiritual crisis, and on the outcome of that crisis
depended the future of the people of God in the
world. It was a moment of decision and a turning
point. In the prophetic interpretation of history,
Israel dies to rise again. In terms of the existing situation, the present Jewish establishment is doomed;
the true people of God will emerge from its ruins.

The idea finds expression in various metaphors—
seldom, if ever, in blunt prose. Most pregnant is a
saying whose precise wording we cannot determine,
because it is handed down in such various forms, but
which, for that very reason, we may safely conclude
to be both authentic and specially significant. Jesus
was reported to have said something about the de-
struction of the temple, and this was made a charge
against him. It was clearly an embarrassment to his
followers in the tense situation that arose after his
death. Mark gives the words thus: "I will throw
down this temple, made with human hands, and in
three days I will build another, not made with
hands." But, Mark says, the allegation was false;
he did not say this. But what did he say? Matthew
has the words somewhat differently but he too discredits the report. Luke just drops it out. John, however, states plainly that Jesus did say: "Destroy this
temple and in three days I will raise it again." [12]
We must, I think, accept John's version of the matter,
and recognize that the saying is, like so many others,

figurative: the temple stands for a way of religion and a community embodying it. The manifest disintegration of the existing system is to be preliminary to the appearance of a new way of religion and a new community to embody it. And yet, it is the *same* temple, first destroyed, that is to be rebuilt. The new community is still Israel; there is continuity through the discontinuity. It is not a matter of replacement but of resurrection.

We have now, perhaps, some inkling of the purpose underlying the intensive campaign which Jesus conducted among the populace of Galilee and Judaea. His aim was to constitute a community worthy of the name of a people of God, a divine commonwealth, through individual response to God coming in his kingdom. Some of his approaches to individuals we have already noted, and the results. Each such case was an image in miniature of the way in which the new people of God is brought into being, for in each case a man is made new by the power of God released through Jesus and through the "faith" which he evoked. Every such case is also a reinforcement of the call to "repentance," and they are all part and parcel of the great campaign.

Behind it all lies the vision of the all-embracing power and benevolence of the Creator. Especially it is the miracle of growth that sets the pattern. A man sows seed, "it sprouts and grows—how, he does not know—the ground produces a crop by itself," and almost before he knows what is happening, "harvest time has come." [13] Accordingly, when Jesus sent out messengers to proclaim, as he had himself proclaimed, "The kingdom of God is upon you," they are represented as reapers: "The crop is heavy, but laborers are scarce; you must therefore beg the owner to send laborers to harvest his crop. Be on your way!" [14] To change the metaphor, they are "fishers of men," [15] and fishers with a dragnet,[16] which gathers in fish of all kinds, without discrimination. It is not for them to pick and choose. The disciples are recruiting agents for the new people of God, but their function as such is simply to confront men with the reality of God coming in his kingdom, and leave it to them. The response of each individual is voluntary; it is a choice and a decision of his own, before God. Those who accept his kingdom "like a child" enter in, and so by act of God himself, which is especially exhibited in the forgiveness of sins, his people is formed within the old Israel, ready to emerge in due time.

If the new Israel was to be more than an abstraction, it needed to be embodied. No doubt it was a theoretical possibility that a reformed Judaism might have supplied such an embodiment. Indeed, after the fall of Jerusalem the new rabbinic Judaism under the guidance of Rabbi Jochanan ben Zakkai and his school undertook something of the kind. But, as we have seen, Jesus did not contemplate a reformed Judaism. Yet he recognized the need for some vehicle of the new life which was emerging. There is a hint of this in a parable: "No one puts new wine into old wineskins; if he does, the wine will burst the skins and then wine and skins are both lost. Fresh skins for new wine!" [17] The fresh vehicle was in fact beginning to take shape. The disciples of Jesus were called to be more than recruiting agents for the people of God, they were to be its foundation members.

This was most definitely true of the inner group which drew together out of the larger body of those who adhered to the cause of Jesus in a general way. It consisted of men who were wholly committed, and had left all to put themselves at his disposal. The number of this inner group came to be fixed at twelve. It seems clear that Jesus himself fixed it so, and, almost certainly, to symbolize the people of Israel with its traditional twelve tribes. In a very bold figure they are represented as "sitting on twelve thrones as judges of the twelve tribes of Israel." [18] They are addressed in terms proper to the people of God as an entity. All through the Old Testament, Israel is the "flock" of God, and so Jesus addresses the Twelve: "Have no fear, little flock; for your Father has chosen to give you the kingdom." [19] They are the Israel-to-be in miniature; not indeed to the exclusion of other disciples; it does not appear that in the gospels the Twelve form anything like a closed corporation. The center of the community is defined clearly enough: it is centered in Jesus and those closest to him; but its boundaries are not drawn. Any who hear his call to "repentance" and accept from his teaching the direction for their "change of mind," are members of the Israel-to-be. It is impossible, on the evidence we have, to distinguish clearly among the ethical sayings those which were delivered to a public audience, or in the course of discussion in a mixed group, or privately to the inner circle. Nor is it necessary to do so. In one aspect they are addressed to all and sundry, laying down the lines of an absolute ethic determined by the coming of the kingdom of God; but insofar as individuals accept them as such, and commit themselves, the new Israel is being formed, and the ethical teaching of Jesus becomes the new law by which it is to be governed.

But over and above the broad ethical teaching, intrinsically universal in its scope, there are sayings addressed directly to the disciples as a community in being, capable of being compared and contrasted with other existing communities: "You know that in the world the recognized rulers lord it over their subjects, and their great men make them feel the weight of authority. That is not the way with you; among you, whoever wants to be great must be your servant, and whoever wants to be first must be the willing slave of all." [20] The theme recurs with striking frequency. Evidently it was, in the mind of Jesus, fundamental to the whole idea of the divine commonwealth. The saying just quoted is said to have been called forth by the appearance of rivalries among the Twelve. We seem to have a glimpse of a group of men striving to become a real community, and blundering through natural human failings. They are enthusiasts; they have given up everything for the cause; that in itself implies a more than average power of concentration on an object. That such men should entertain a not ignoble ambition to be leaders in the community can easily be understood. Nor was it wrong to seek leadership, provided it was the leadership of service. Any other form of the ambition to be first was directly contrary to the very idea of the people of God as Jesus conceived it. On one occasion he is reported to have enforced the lesson by example, when he took upon himself the duty (which in most households was performed by a slave) of washing the feet of his company.[21] "Who is the greater," he asked, "the one who sits at table, or the servant who waits on him? Surely the one who sits at table. Yet here am I among you like a servant." [22] We should understand this idea of the primacy of selfless service as applying not only to the relations of individuals within the community, but also to the function of the community in the world. The "messianic" idea as popularly held meant both the rule of the Messiah over Israel and also the domination of Israel over the nations. The new Israel has a "Messiah" who is the servant of all, and it must find itself in the like way of service.

The full scope of the demand made on the Twelve as the nucleus of the new community comes into view at the point when Jesus decided to lead them to Jerusalem, where by this time opposition had consolidated in the seats of power. It was clear that in going there he was putting his head into the lion's mouth. Those who accompanied him must be under no illusion. Commitment to his cause now meant even more than it had done when they were called to leave home and livelihood. "If anyone comes to me and does not hate his father and mother, wife and children, brothers and sisters, *even his own life*, he cannot be a disciple of mine. No one who does not carry his cross and come with me can be a disciple of mine." [23] So Luke has it. Matthew gives the saying in slightly different terms: "No man is worthy of me who cares more for father or mother than for me; no man is worthy of me who cares more for son or daughter; no man is worthy of me who does not take up his cross and walk in my footsteps." [24]

Most likely Jesus deliberately chose the harsh and extreme language which we find in Luke. It is in the tone of the occasion. He was calling for volunteers who renounce everything, renounce ("hate") life itself. And this renunciation of life is expressed again, in the most harshly realistic terms. To "carry the cross" is no mere metaphor. Crucifixion was the Romans' short way with rebels. A criminal condemned to this atrocious punishment was normally compelled to carry to the place of execution the crossbeam to which he was to be fastened. That is the picture which the words of Jesus conjured up in the minds of those who heard him. They were to go to

Jerusalem like a procession of condemned criminals with halters round their necks. Such was to be the end of the journey for him; he invited them to share it. "Can you drink the cup that I drink," he asked, "and be baptized with the baptism I am baptized with?" "We can," they replied.[25]

It should be noted that the call to "carry the cross" is addressed to those who volunteered for service on a particular occasion. Jesus did not expect all those who had come to him in faith to accompany him on this desperate venture nor, if they did not do so, did he mean to disqualify them for a part in the new community. But the principle upon which the call is based is a universal one: "Whoever cares for his own safety is lost; but if a man will let himself be lost for my sake and for the gospel, that man is safe."[26]

John has given this saying in a peculiarly suggestive setting. We have seen how central to the ideal of the emergence of the people of God is the thought expressed in the parables of seed and harvest. John has another such parable, in which the thought takes a deeper turn: "A grain of wheat remains a solitary grain unless it falls into the ground and dies; but if it dies, it bears a rich harvest";[27] and then, with an echo of Luke's language about "hating" one's own life, "The man who loves himself is lost, but he who hates himself [in this world] will be kept safe [for eternal life]." Renunciation of self is the principle that validates the total commitment to God and his kingdom which Jesus demanded. In circumstances which put it to the utmost test, it might find expression in actual martyrdom, but something of its quality must be present in all truly ethical action. We have seen that the whole conception of a new people of God is based upon the principle of "dying to live," and here we have a model of the Israel-to-be as it shaped itself in the company of the followers of Jesus. In them the people of God was to die in order to live again.

The march on Jerusalem ended, as Jesus had foreseen, in a situation of intense conflict. As it reached its climax, he gathered the Twelve for a solemn meal together. At the close of the meal he passed round a cup of wine with the words, "This cup is the new covenant sealed with my blood" [28]—these or similar words, for they are handed down in somewhat varying forms. There will be more to be said about this pregnant utterance, but for the moment it is the term "covenant" that concerns us. It was the postulate of the Jewish religion that the status of Israel as the people of God was founded upon a "covenant" which bound them to his service. When complete collapse came in the sixth century B.C., a prophet had spoken of a "new covenant" as the basis of the new Israel that was to arise from the ruins of the old.[29] In the time of Jesus the sectaries of Qumran regarded themselves as the people of the new covenant. The idea, therefore, of a covenant as the foundation charter (so to speak) of the people of God was very much alive at the time, and there can be no doubt what Jesus had in mind when he invited his followers to drink of the cup of the covenant: he was formally installing them as foundation members of the new people of God.

And yet before the night was over they deserted him; he was arrested and brought to trial, and they scattered and left him to his fate. The new Israel seemed to have melted away at its very inception. And this raises an acute historical problem: how was it, in these circumstances, that the Christian Church ever got going at all? The answer that the first Christians gave (and who could know better than

they?) was that Jesus returned to them, alive after
death, and that this return was an act of forgiveness,
which reinstated them in the place they had forfeited
by their disloyalty. This is movingly portrayed in a
dramatic scene at the end of the Fourth Gospel,
where Peter meets the risen Jesus on the lake shore,
after a night's fruitless fishing. Peter, we have been
told, had emphatically and even brutally dissociated
himself from his Master at the time of his trial. After
that, Peter never again saw him alive until that
morning by the lake, when, unexpectedly, incredibly,
they met again. Part of the conversation which followed must be transcribed in John's words: "After
breakfast, Jesus said to Simon Peter, 'Simon son of
John, do you love me?' 'Yes, Lord,' he answered,
'You know I love you.' 'Then tend my sheep.' . . .
Then he added, 'Follow me.' " [30] In those words
the deserter is brought back to the very beginning
and given a fresh start, his disloyalty blotted out.
It is a picture of what happened to the "little
flock" in which the new people of God was embodied.
It had indeed melted away, and there was nothing
to show for all the work that had been done, until it
was re-created by an act of forgiveness. This was the
emergence of the new Israel, of which the prophets
had spoken in terms of resurrection from the grave.
That was how the church was brought into existence, and it could never forget that its foundation
members were discredited men who owed their position solely to the magnanimity of their ill-used
Master.

VI

THE MESSIAH

In an historical view, the one evident outcome of the whole life and work of Jesus was the emergence of the church, a society which regarded itself as carrying on the distinctive vocation of Israel as the "people of God," and yet was quite clear that it was a *new* Israel, constituted by a "new covenant." It had taken shape, not about a platform or a creed, but about a personal attachment to Jesus himself.

The relation in which he stood to the new Israel was defined in the early church by assigning to him the traditional title, "Messiah," the "Anointed." For Greek-speaking people this was literally translated as "Christos," Christ; but even so it was not generally understood, and it was soon taken to be simply a proper name. But in the gospels generally the term is fully alive in something like its original sense, and we shall do well to retain the Hebrew word as a reminder that "Christ," or "Messiah," is here neither a personal name nor a theological term, but an index to an historical role. John, in bringing his gospel to a close, says it was written to support the belief that "Jesus is the Messiah." [1] The writers

of the other gospels might have said as much. It is all
the more surprising that in the account they give of
his words and actions the use of the title is comparatively scanty, and there is some ambiguity about it.
Except in one passage of the Fourth Gospel,[2] Jesus
is never represented as spontaneously claiming, in so
many words, to be Messiah, and even there it is not
a public claim. Not only so; he seems to have dis-
couraged attempts on the part of others to give him
the title, though he may not always have been in a
position to silence them. In two instances only he
appears, somewhat doubtfully, to have accepted it.

The first occasion, as described in the three earlier
gospels, finds Jesus alone with his closest followers
at a place outside the boundaries of Jewish Palestine,
known as Caesarea Philippi. Jesus asked his disciples
to tell him what people were saying about him. They
gave some answers. Then he asked, "And you, who
do you say I am?" Peter replied, "You are the
Messiah." From this point our informants diverge.
According to Mark (closely followed by Luke), all the
response that Peter got was: "he gave them strict
orders not to tell anyone about him." Matthew gives
a different view. As he has it, Jesus welcomed Peter's
statement, and yet, after praising him, went on (in
agreement with Mark's account) to warn them
against letting anyone hear them say that he was
Messiah. In John (to complete our survey) we seem to
be looking at the same scene, perhaps through a less
transparent medium, and yet one which allows us to
see its main outlines. According to John, Peter did
not actually use the term "Messiah," but said, "We
know that you are the Holy One of God." The difference may be verbal: "anointing" (which makes
the Messiah) is consecration, and the person so consecrated is "holy," by definition. There is something

strangely enigmatic about this scene. Did Jesus, or
did he not, intend to accept the title? If we follow
Matthew, he did, though with some reservation. If
we follow Mark, Luke and John, the most we can
say is that he did not refuse it.[3]

And now let us look at the other occasion. According to the three earlier gospels, when Jesus was
brought up for examination before the High Priest,
he was asked point-blank, "Are you the Messiah?"
According to Mark he replied, without ambiguity,
"I am." According to Matthew the reply was, "The
words are yours" (literally, "You have said"; there
is no sufficient evidence that this was an accepted
form of affirmation, either in Greek or in Hebrew
or Aramaic; we might paraphrase it, "You may have
it so if you choose"). In Luke we read that Jesus refused to reply at all. "Tell us, are you the Messiah?"
says the High Priest; Jesus retorts, "If I tell you,
you will not believe me." John does not describe
the scene before the High Priest, but there seem
to be echoes of it in a passage where Jesus is publicly
challenged in words similar to those of Luke: "If
you are the Messiah, say so plainly." Jesus replies,
"I have told you but you do not believe" (meaning,
apparently, that various things he had said and done
should have led them to the right answer).[4] Here
again we have the same problem: did Jesus, or did
he not, when he was publicly questioned, intend
to accept the title, "Messiah"?

We may perhaps get some light on the matter if
we consider the sequel to this questioning. Whether
it was at a formal examination in court, or earlier
in a public confrontation, that Jesus was asked the
crucial question, we may fairly understand it as a
preliminary to his arraignment before the Roman
governor. The charge which was then preferred by

the priests was that of claiming to be "king of the
Jews." The charge was of course framed for Roman
ears. Among themselves the priests would not have
used that expression. They would have said that
he claimed falsely to be the "anointed" king of Israel,
the Messiah. In his examination before Pilate Jesus
was asked, "Are you the king of the Jews?" and he
replied (as all gospels agree) with the noncommittal
expression, "The words are yours" ("Have it so if
you choose"). At this juncture a refusal to disown the
title would have the same effect as an avowal, and
it was a matter of life and death. Jesus at any rate
allowed himself to be condemned to death for claiming to be (in Jewish terms) Messiah.[5]

As we have seen, the office of Messiah was conceived
in various ways, but always it was bound up with the
special calling and destiny of Israel as the people of
God. From the gospels we gather that Jesus set himself to constitute the new Israel under his own leadership; he nominated its foundation members, and
admitted them into the new "covenant," and he laid
down its new law. That was his mission. If it did not
entirely agree with any of the contemporary ideas
of what the Messiah should do, there was no other
term available which came near to covering it. He
could not deny his mission; he could not disavow the
authority that went with it; and therefore, if the
question was posed, he could not simply repudiate
the title "Messiah." But it was an embarrassment to
him, and he preferred that it should not be used
publicly, until at last his hand was forced. In the
popular mind messiahship was associated with the
political and military role of the "Son of David."
To play that part was the last thing Jesus desired.
Any suggestion that he proposed to do so was a
hindrance to his true work and a danger to his cause.

His appeal to his people must rest on something other than a debatable claim to messiahship.

Yet a title which he would not deny to save his life cannot have been without significance for him. Messiah he was, in his own sense of the term. We may therefore reframe our question, and ask, not, "Did Jesus claim to be Messiah?" but, "What kind of Messiah did he intend to be?" He would not be the Messiah of popular expectation. What then? At Caesarea Philippi, Peter hailed Jesus as Messiah. Jesus, having warned his followers not to say anything of the sort in public, abruptly changed the subject, or so it appeared to them: "He began to teach them that the Son of Man had to undergo great sufferings and to be rejected." (The enigmatic expression "Son of Man" we will leave for later discussion; here we may take it to mean simply "I.") Peter was scandalized, and took it upon him to set his Master right on the point. "Heaven forbid! No, Lord, this shall never happen to you." Jesus retorted in terms of unwonted asperity. "Away with you, tempter! You think as men think, not as God thinks." [6] Beneath the sharp interchange lies a profound difference of view. To Peter, this talk of suffering and rejection was utterly incongruous with any idea of messiahship; and most Jews of his time would have agreed with him. The Messiah was to be a conqueror, not a sufferer, not rejected but acclaimed as king of Israel. So the scriptures appeared to affirm.

They might however have recalled that the Old Testament knew of another character, hardly less significant than the Messiah himself, whose role was essentially that of the innocent sufferer. This character appears especially in certain passages in the latter part of the Book of Isaiah,[7] as the "Servant of the Lord." To summarize briefly, he is one who has

H

been given and has accepted a calling from God, and devoted himself body and soul to his service, bearing witness to the truth of God, enduring many sufferings, and in the end laying down his life for the sake of others. When the early church came to grips with the problem presented by the extraordinary career and the tragic fate of its Founder, it turned for elucidation to these passages of Isaiah, which speak of a life of service and a martyr's death.

Matthew, indeed, has taken over the passage where Isaiah first introduces the figure of the Servant, and attached it as a kind of motto to his account of the mission of Jesus:

> "Here is my Servant, whom I have chosen,
> my beloved, on whom my favour rests;
> I will put my spirit upon him,
> and he will proclaim judgment among the nations.
> He will not strive, he will not shout,
> nor will his voice be heard in the streets.
> He will not snap off the broken reed,
> nor snuff out the smouldering wick,
> until he leads justice on to victory.
> In him the nations shall place their hope." [8]

In particular, the Servant is commissioned "to bring Jacob back to the Lord, and that Israel should be gathered to him"; [9] and so Jesus is said to have declared himself "sent to the lost sheep of the house of Israel." [10] And in fact, as we shall see, this is a key to much of his activity. It explains the importance he attached to his approach to the "tax-gatherers and sinners," in whom he saw just such "lost sheep." And if the mission of the Servant defined the work to which Jesus set his hand, the fate of the Servant, whose life was made "an offering for sin," [11] and who "bore the sin of many," pointed to the destiny that awaited him: "The Son of Man came not to be served but to serve, and to give up his life as a ransom for many." [12] There is good reason to think that Jesus himself first directed the attention of his followers to the figure of the Servant. He did so because by reflecting on it they might be led to a juster idea of what it was to be "Messiah." "You think as men think, not as God thinks," he said to Peter; we might venture to paraphrase: "Your Messiah is a conqueror; God's Messiah is a servant."

The fusion of the two ideal figures of Messiah and Servant of the Lord in the historical person of Jesus is dramatically represented in the scene which in all gospels prefaces the story of his public career. Let us take Mark's account. Jesus has been baptized in the River Jordan. "At the moment when he came up out of the water he saw the heavens torn open and the Spirit, like a dove, descending upon him. And a voice spoke from heaven: 'You are my Son, my Beloved; on you my favor rests.' " [13] Obviously all this is symbolic. If we want to decode the symbolism we may start with the words spoken by the "voice from heaven." They come out of the Old Testament. "You are my Son" was addressed to the king of Israel, prototype of the Messiah.[14] "My beloved on whom my favor rests" is the Servant of the Lord in the prophecy of Isaiah.[15] There the Servant is equipped for his task by the gift of the Spirit, which is here symbolized by the open heavens and the descent of the dove. Here then is a summary of the essential purport of the life and work of Jesus in a kind of symbolic shorthand: he undertook his mission, our informants are saying, as Messiah, as Son of God, as the Servant of the Lord, in the power of the divine Spirit—and this is "God's truth," affirmed by the divine voice whose echo can be caught by the inward ear.

If however we conclude that Jesus saw his mission adumbrated in the ideal figure of the Servant of the Lord, we encounter a certain difficulty. The mission of the Servant, his demeanor, actions and sufferings, are depicted in vividly personal terms, and yet we repeatedly come upon such expressions as "Israel, thou art my servant," or "Jacob my servant and Israel my chosen." [16] The alternation between the Servant as individual and the Servant as community is perplexing, but it should not be dismissed as if it were merely confused thinking due, perhaps, to an inability to form a clear idea of the nature of personality. The prophet's description, read with some imagination, suggests the fruitful idea that God is to be worthily served, not by individuals in isolation, but by a community, and yet a community so completely united in his service that it can be spoken of as a person. It may even suggest that it is possible to conceive a real person in whom the corporate unity finds effective expression. Nor is this idea so farfetched as it might seem at first sight. After all, history, and even recent history, knows instances where a powerful personality, temporarily and for particular ends, has come to embody in himself the spirit and purpose of a whole nation, and has been spontaneously recognized as its representative, in a more than formal sense. We may legitimately have such an analogy in mind when the gospels present Jesus in terms proper to the Servant of the Lord. The Messiah is not only founder and leader of the Israel-to-be, the new people of God; he is its "inclusive representative." In a real sense he *is* the true Israel, carrying through in his own experience the process through which it comes into being.

It is in this sense that we may read the remarkable passage which, in the three earlier gospels, follows immediately upon the scene of the baptism. We are still in the realm of dramatic symbolism. Jesus is represented as engaged in a controversy with the devil, who suggests to him various courses of action. Each suggestion is countered by a quotation of Scripture; by a quotation, to be precise, from the Book of Deuteronomy.[17] Let us then look there for a key to the meaning of the scene. Moses is addressing the Israelites toward the end of their wanderings in the wilderness:

> Remember all the road by which the Lord your God led you these forty years in the wilderness, to humble you and put you to the test, to see whether you were minded to keep his commandments or not. He humbled you and famished you with hunger, and then fed you with manna, which your fathers never knew, to teach you that man cannot live on bread alone, but lives on every word that God utters.

And now look at what Matthew writes:

> Jesus was then led away by the Spirit into the wilderness to be tested by the devil. For forty days and nights he fasted, and at the end of them he was famished. The tempter approached him and said, "If you are the Son of God, tell these stones to become bread." Jesus answered, "Scripture says, 'Man cannot live on bread alone; he lives on every word that God utters.' "

And so the story continues. At each stage we are reminded of incidents in which Israel was tested in the wilderness, and now the Israel-to-be, in the person of the Messiah (the Servant of the Lord) is put to the test. But where ancient Israel failed to pass the test, he stands firm. What may lie behind the story by way of a personal experience is a question I shall raise later; but our informants are telling us that Jesus won his victory, not simply for himself as an individual, but as the representative of the people of God incorporate in him.

Such "representation" might of course be no more than a legal, or even a literary, fiction. But here we can see that it was given reality by an actual and deliberate self-identification with people. This is the meaning of such sayings as "Anything you did for one of my brothers here, you did it for me," [18] or "Whoever receives one such child in my name receives me." [19] With this clue, we can see why his reporters give such prominence to the association of Jesus with the rejected, and his compassionate approach to the suffering and frustrated. He was creating a solidarity between himself and those whom he saw as being, by grace of God, members of the Israel-to-be, even though the existing "Israel" (the Jewish establishment) might not recognize them. In this light also we can see that when he called disciples to follow him he was both recruiting them into the new community and (which was the same thing) inviting them to identify themselves with him. Such identity he asserted when he sent them out to carry forward his own mission: "To receive you is to receive me." [20] It meant also sharing his lot: "The cup that I drink you shall drink, and the baptism I am baptised with shall be your baptism." [21]

The symbol of a "cup" to be drunk recurs. As we have seen, at their last supper together, he handed his disciples a cup of wine, with the words, "This cup is the new covenant sealed by my blood" (or,

as otherwise reported, "This is my blood of the covenant, shed for many.").[22] He was alluding to the ancient custom by which a solemn agreement or under-
taking was validated by the sacrifice of an animal.
But in the Judaism of the first century, although the
primitive rite of animal sacrifice lingered on (until
the temple was destroyed in A.D. 70), the language
associated with it had taken on meanings proper to
religion on a more developed and spiritual level.
Such language is employed in the prophetic description of the Servant of the Lord who died for others;
and similarly the Jewish martyrs who suffered in the
time of the Maccabees were said to have offered
themselves as a sacrifice for the nation. Thus the
idea of sacrifice passed into that of *self*-sacrifice, as a
personal and moral act. Jesus was saying that in
order that the "covenant" might become effective,
or in other words that the new people of God might
come into existence, he was voluntarily taking a
course which would lead to his death. This was the
length to which he was prepared to go in identifying
himself with those to whom his mission was directed.
The sharing in the cup by the disciples was a demonstration of their solidarity with their Master, both
as beneficiaries of his sacrifice, and as being themselves committed to a like self-devotion for others,
for this belongs to the character of the true people
of God.

It was on the same occasion that Jesus spoke
words which came to stand as the pre-eminent expression of this principle of solidarity. "During supper,"
we read, "he took bread, and having said the bless-
ing he broke it and gave it to them, with the words,
'Take this; this is my body.'" [23] No words of his are
more firmly attested. The breadth and depth of their
implications is a matter that has exercised the minds

of Christian thinkers from the beginning until now. It is not necessary here to go into all that. But it is worthwhile to recall that within the first generation it was possible for Paul not only to describe the "breaking of bread" at the fellowship meal of Christians as "sharing in the body of Christ," [24] but to pass on from that to the idea that the church (the new Israel as it emerged in history) is itself the "body of Christ," each member of which is "in Christ," as Christ is "in him." The language, it appears, is Paul's own invention, but he invented it to describe something that was there before ever he became a Christian at all. It goes back to the solidarity of Jesus with those for whom he gave his life, and their identification with him. This, we may believe, consistently with the whole trend of his teaching, lay behind his words and actions when he gave his disciples bread and said, "This is my body." The church recalled it, from the beginning, in dramatic action; and in this it was wise, or fortunate, for a doctrine of "representation," or "corporate personality," may well appear abstruse; but those who share the broken bread in Christian fellowship know in themselves what it means, whether or not they could form, or accept, any particular theory about it.

In a number of the significant sayings we have been considering, we meet with the peculiar expression, "Son of Man." [25] It is now time to ask what meaning we are to attach to it. The question has been much debated, and it cannot be said to have found an agreed answer. I can only offer what has come to seem to me the most probable way of understanding it. To begin with, there is no sufficient evidence that in Jewish circles of the time of Jesus "Son of Man" was current as a title equivalent, or alternative, to "Messiah," or indeed as a title at all. The expression, as unnatural in Greek as it is in English, is a literal translation from the Aramaic which was the native speech of Jesus and his first followers. In Aramaic, "son-of-man" is a quite ordinary way of saying "man," in the sense of an individual of the human species ("a man," or "the man," as the case may be). The writers of the gospels must have had some particular reason for translating it with an almost wooden literalness. It is noteworthy that they do so only in reporting sayings of Jesus. They never place this particular expression in the mouth of any other speaker, nor do they use it in telling their stories. It may be that they have sometimes introduced it into sayings where Jesus did not use it, but the most likely reason for this surely is that it was felt to be characteristic of the way in which he was accustomed to speak. What was his intention?

In many of the sayings, "Son of Man" could be replaced by "I" or "me" without apparent change of meaning. In other sayings it might seem as if he were referring to someone other than himself. Now in the Aramaic of Palestine it was not uncommon for a speaker, on occasion, to substitute "son-of-man" (i.e., "a man," or "the man") for the first personal pronoun. He might do so out of a certain sensitiveness in speaking about himself, or a desire to avoid the appearance of egotism. (We might compare the affectation, in colloquial English, of saying "one" in place of a blunt "I.") Or he might have a particular reason for using some reserve and leaving a possible doubt whether he really meant himself or "so-and-so." Thus, if a similar doubt can arise (as it has arisen) regarding some of the sayings of Jesus, there is nothing inherently strange about it, in a speaker of Aramaic. Only, we have to ask whether it is possible to discern any particular reason why, in certain connections, he should have chosen this indirect form of speech. I think it is possible. There are sayings so astonishingly bold that their very boldness might seem to justify the avoidance of direct statement in the first person. Some of these will come up for notice presently. But both there and elsewhere the use of the indirect form might often be understood if Jesus wished to suggest, without saying it in so many words, that he was fulfilling a role which would be recognized by those sensitive to his message, while others would be left asking (as John says they did ask), "What son-of-man is this?" [26] If so, then it would appear that the role he wished to suggest was that of the prophetic Servant of the Lord, with its overtones of corporate representation, which, as we have seen, was so much in his mind.

It is at any rate striking that so many of the "Son of Man" sayings are associated with functions of the Servant, and especially where Jesus is referring to the sufferings and death that lie before him: "The Son of Man is to undergo great sufferings . . . to be rejected . . . to be treated with contempt"; "The Son of Man came to give up his life as a ransom for many." [27] All of these echo the language of the prophet. The forecasts are more than an intelligent reading of the existing situation and its likely developments, though in part they may be just that; they are the acceptance of a vocation, and there is a solemnity about them to which the more indirect mode of speech might seem appropriate. If Jesus thus employed a familiar way of speaking, not just casually but in circumstances which made it the vehicle of a partly veiled assertion of his vocation, then "Son of Man" came to be something like a self-designation replacing the traditional title of "Messiah." That is how the writers of the gospels seem to have understood it. ⫽

Some of the forecasts to which I have referred point to a destiny lying beyond suffering and death. Of this Jesus is reported to have spoken in various ways. Some sayings speak of "rising from the dead," some speak of "coming again," and sometimes they are in vaguer terms: "A little while and you see me no more; again a little while and you will see me." [28] It is perhaps impossible to decide which of these best represent what Jesus actually said. That forecasts may have grown more specific in the light of what happened is likely enough. It is also likely enough that what he said on various occasions was sometimes more explicit, sometimes more cryptic. But one thing we may say with reasonable certainty: quite apart from the question of the authenticity or the verbal accuracy of this or that reported saying, the idea of new life through death, of victory coming out of defeat, is an inseparable part of the thought of Jesus about his destiny.

So much we may be content to affirm. Beyond that there are difficulties to be encountered. If we go back to the three types of forecast which I have distinguished, we may say that "rising from the dead" speaks simply of life beyond the grave, and "a little while and you will see me" speaks of the renewal of personal relations interrupted by death. These are tolerably straightforward. But the language about the coming of the Son of Man is another matter. "The Son of Man is to come in the glory of his Father"; "They will see the Son of Man coming in the clouds"; "Like the lightning flash that lights up the earth from end to end, will the Son of Man be when his day comes." [29] Of course it is imaginative symbolism; but what does it symbolize? It occurs in association with language about the Last Judgment and the End of the World, which apparently are conceived (at least in some passages) to coincide with the coming of the Son of Man. We cannot but recognize here traits of the "apocalyptic" hopes and speculations which, with a long ancestry behind them, revived in strength during the feverish years that preceded the fall of Jerusalem. The early Christians shared many of these hopes. They discussed them anxiously, as we know from writings of the New Testament outside the gospels. We can understand that they seized avidly upon any remembered words of their Lord which seemed to have a bearing upon them.

They remembered, for example, that he had uttered somber warnings of disasters threatening the Jewish community and its holy city, and that he had said that "this generation" was doomed to bear the accumulated guilt of Israel's sinful past. Perhaps (they thought) he was really saying that in the lifetime of men and women about him God's final judgment would bring history to a close, so that "this generation" would actually be the last of all. There are passages in the gospels which seem to say so. Is this what Jesus meant? Or should we be right in suspecting that his reporters, understandably anxious to find his words relevant to their own urgent preoccupations, have given them a twist away from their original intention? There is reason to believe they have sometimes done so.

Yet we should here proceed with caution. It is reasonable to suppose that Jesus himself would have employed the imagery which was traditional and familiar among his contemporaries. Only, as I observed earlier, while the imagery was largely inherited, it could be, and was, applied differently by different people. If Jesus did use it, it does not follow, either that he intended it to be taken literally, or that he meant by it just what his reporters supposed. The question remains open, what did he mean?

It would seem right to start from the standpoint of sayings which are both plain and central to the teaching of Jesus. Nothing in it is more clearly original or characteristic than his declaration that the kingdom of God is here. It meant that a hope has become a reality. You no longer look for the reign of God through a telescope; you open your eyes to see. But at the same time there is more than meets the eye. It is the reign *of God;* it is the eternal God himself, here present. There is a power at work in this world which is not of this world, something "super-natural," an invasion from the Beyond—however you may choose to express it. It gives an eternal dimension to the temporal present, and to each succeeding "present"; but it can never be exhausted in any temporal present, however deeply significant. The kingdom of God, while it is present experience, remains also a hope, but a hope directed to a consummation beyond history.

To express this aspect of the kingdom Jesus was content to make use of long-established symbols—a feast with the blessed dead who are "alive to God," [30] a great assize with "all nations" standing at the bar.[31] These are not forthcoming events, to which a date might be assigned. They stand as symbols for the reality to which the spirit of man awakes when it is done with past, present and future. This is the kingdom of God in the fulness of its meaning, and it lies beyond history. And yet it "came" in history, in that crucial episode of which Jesus was himself the active center. Its blessedness was a present possession of those who accepted it. "How blest are you who are poor! The kingdom of God is yours." [32] They were guests at a wedding feast: "How can you expect the bridegroom's friends to fast while the bridegroom is with them?" [33] And yet, it is in another world than this that they are to "eat and drink at his, table in his kingdom." [34] Again, the moment of decision to which the presence of Jesus brought those who encountered him was the judgment inseparable from the coming of the kingdom. *"Now,"* writes John, "is the hour of judgment for this world" [35]—the Last Judgment, he means. Essentially it was a judgment which people passed on themseives by their reaction to his presence. It might be acquittal ("Your faith has saved you. Go in peace.") [36] or it might be condemnation ("Alas for you! It will be more bearable for Sodom on the Day of Judgment.").[37] It is judgment in history, but its significance reaches beyond history; and this ultra-historical significance is expressed in the dramatic picture of all nations gathered before the throne of the heavenly Judge.

In view of this, it follows that the total event of the earthly career of Jesus, as well as his action in detail, is regarded in two aspects: on the one side it had effects in an actual historical situation; on the other side it had a significance reaching out into man's eternal destiny, and to be expressed only in symbol.

It is in this light, I suggest, that we may best understand the cryptic sayings about the coming of the Son of Man. Central to the whole group of such sayings is the answer which Jesus is reported to have given to the High Priest when he was interrogated about his alleged messianic pretensions: "You will see the Son of Man seated at the right hand of God

and coming with the clouds of heaven." [38] The language is allusive and the imagery close-packed. There
are echoes of two passages in the Old Testament. In
one of these the Almighty is represented as conferring the highest dignity on the king of Israel (prototype of the Messiah), in the words, "Sit at my right
hand." [39] This is here associated with another passage, from the Book of Daniel, which describes, in
bizarre imagery, a vision of things to come. First,
there is a procession of weird and ferocious beasts,
and then "one like a son-of-man [a human form, as
distinct from the bestial figures] came with the
clouds of heaven," to be invested with everlasting
dominion.[40] The prophet himself has supplied a
key. The beasts stand for the brutal pagan empires
by which Israel had been successively oppressed, and
the human figure stands for "the people of the saints
of the Most High." He is therefore a "double" of the
Servant of the Lord, an embodiment of the people
of God, first oppressed and then vindicated in glory.
It is a vision of the final victory of God's cause over
all powers in the universe; it is also a vision of
(expected) historical victory for Israel over its op-
pressors. We are probably to understand that in
recalling this prophecy Jesus also was pointing to
the final victory of God's cause, or in other words the
consummation of his kingdom, beyond history, and
was affirming his own part in it; but as in Daniel, so
here, this victory has its embodiment in history,
namely in the impending fate of Jesus himself, who
is to pass through suffering and sacrifice to glorious
life. The human figure of Daniel's vision has acquired a new identity. It is this historical Person in
whom, as its "inclusive representative," the new
Israel, the people of God, is to emerge from apparently irretrievable disaster—"raised to life with

Christ," as Paul was to express it.[41] This is the coming of the Son of Man on the historical plane. His ultimate "coming" lies beyond history, but the essential pattern of it is already given in the historical Person and the historical event.

VII

THE STORY:[1]
(I) GALILEE

Philip, a galilean from Bethsaida, came across a friend somewhere in Transjordan, and proposed to introduce him to another Galilean who had made a great impression on him, "Jesus son of Joseph, from Nazareth." "Nazareth!" Nathanael exclaimed, "Can anything good come from Nazareth?"[2] The vivid little scene, whether or not it is strictly historical, places Jesus in his contemporary setting. The kind of environment in which he grew up can be described out of his own parables. Read with attention they yield a composite portrait of a whole community going about its daily affairs.[3] Looking at the picture we may ask from what standpoint within this society it is observed. The answer is plain: it is that of the *petit bourgeois,* small farmer or independent craftsman, equally removed from the well-to-do and the "proletariat." To this class, we must conclude, the family of Jesus belonged. If at a later stage he was poor and homeless, this was a voluntary poverty, embraced for ideal ends. His most intimate associates, or at any rate those about whom we are told the most, were partners in a fishery business, owning their own boats and employing labor. Jesus himself, Mark says, was a carpenter; the son of a carpenter, says Matthew. Such crafts were normally hereditary. There is a parable about a son learning his trade by watching his father at work: "A son can do nothing on his own account, but only what he sees his father doing. What the father does, the son does in the same manner. For the father loves his son and shows him everything that he does himself" (all the secrets of the craft).[4] It is perhaps not too bold to find here a reminiscence of the family workshop at Nazareth. There Jesus learned to be a "carpenter"; but the word in Greek (and in the native Aramaic of Galilee) had a wider meaning. His work included, for example, building operations. In one parable he depicts a scene in a carpenter's shop, where two brothers are at work and one of them gets a speck of sawdust in his eye. In another he pillories the jerry-builder who scamps his foundations; and in yet another he notes the importance of drawing up an estimate before operations begin: "Would any of you think of building a tower without first sitting down and calculating the cost, to see whether he could afford to finish it?" The practical craftsman is speaking. Jesus was not only (as we have seen) an observer of the workaday scene; he had been busy in it himself. It should perhaps be added that to say he was a craftsman earning his living is not to say that he was uneducated. The level of literacy among the Jews was probably higher than in any comparable community within the Empire. And although superior persons in Jerusalem dismissed him as "this untrained man," he appears to have been quite capable of meeting scholars learned in the Scriptures upon their own ground.

How long he continued to work at his trade we do not know. The occasion for his breaking away seems clear: it was the appearance on the scene of John son of Zacharias, called the Baptist. This, according to Luke, was in the fifteenth year of the emperor Tiberius, A.D. 28/29, and Jesus was about thirty years of age. This may be taken as a reasonable approxition, though the figures cannot be pressed too closely.

John the Baptist, says the Jewish historian Josephus, was "a good man who commanded the Jews to practise virtue and to be just to one another and devout towards God." [5] So he did, and his moral precepts, so far as they are (scantily) recorded, are practical and down to earth. But Josephus has made it all sound too tame. The impact that John made did not depend on trite exhortations to be good. This formidable ascetic, haunting the wilderness in his uncouth garments, revived the popular image of an inspired prophet, and like the ancient prophets he announced the impending judgment of God on a recreant people. The "Coming One," he said, would soon be here, a terrifying figure, like a woodman laying about him with his axe, like a winnower separating grain from chaff. Indeed (and it was this that gave John's preaching its bite) he was here already, unknown, biding his time.[6] At any moment the axe might fall. John's mission was to warn anyone who would listen to "escape from the coming retribution." What was the way of escape? To confess their sins, "repent," and be baptized.

The rite of baptism, or immersion in water, was no innovation. Various kinds of ritual washings or bathings were widely practised. The sectaries of Qumran had made them into an elaborate system. But John's baptism was different. It was a single, unrepeatable act of initiation. It was more like the

ritual bath which converts to Judaism had to take
before they could be admitted into the holy people,
as a sign that they were purified from the "unclean-
ness" of heathen ways. And now John urged born
Jews, "children of Abraham," to undergo the same
rite of purification, because in his view they needed
it just as much. His task was, says Luke, "to prepare
a people that shall be fit for the Lord." That was
what he was doing when he urged moral reformation
and baptized those who were ready to commit themselves to it. By immersing them in the river Jordan
he marked them for future membership of the "people fit for the Lord." But baptism in water, he insisted, was only preparatory. The Coming One would
"baptize with spirit and fire"—a strongly emotive
phrase which we need not try to spell out. Meanwhile they were to mend their ways and wait—but
not for long.

The response was remarkable. The official representatives of religion, it is true, looked askance, but
masses of people of all sorts and conditions, from
every part of Palestine, flocked to the banks of the
Jordan, including, we are told, soldiers, tax-gatherers
and prostitutes. Among the crowds was Jesus of
Nazareth. What led him to take this step we are not
told. If we have in mind his concern for the rise of
a new people of God out of the confusions of contemporary Judaism, we can see that so far at least
he would be in sympathy with the Baptist's aims.
We have noted how he valued solidarity with those
whom he saw as potential members of the new
Israel, however alienated they might be from the religious establishment. And here they were, pressing
forward to commit themselves, by a public act, to just
such potential membership. Without attempting to
penetrate deeper, we can understand that he would

be impelled to put himself alongside these pathetic crowds—soldiers, tax-gatherers, prostitutes, and all—who confessed their sins and wanted to belong to "a people fit for the Lord."

But at his baptism something happened which altered the current of his life. All four gospels offer some description, heavily weighted, as we have seen, with symbolism. We are entitled to infer that this was the moment at which Jesus accepted his vocation. For him, and not only for those who wrote about him, it was the act of God by which he was "anointed" for his mission.

It is not surprising to be told that the next step was a temporary withdrawal into solitude.[7] The description which the gospels give of that time of withdrawal is, as we have seen, once again highly symbolic. What they are saying is that as Israel was put to the test in the wilderness, so the new Israel, in the person of its Messiah, was put to the test, and came through successfully where the old Israel had failed. Yet for Jesus it was, we may believe, the solution of a personal problem. How was his newly embraced vocation to be carried through, in a situation as full of menace as of opportunity? Some courses of action might suggest themselves with a plausible appeal. He might gain power by "doing homage to the devil," as it is here expressed, or, in realistic terms, exploiting the latent forces of violence to wrest from Rome the liberation of his people. Later, as we shall see, there was a moment when he might have been tempted to do so. Or he might captivate the multitude by an exhibition miracle (for example, said the devil, by throwing himself down from the parapet of the temple and challenging God to intervene). He was in fact later invited to do something of the kind, and refused. His mission was to be guided all through by principles which can be stated very simply, as they are stated here in the three replies to the devil's suggestions. They are: implicit obedience to the will of God ("living on every word that God utters"), trust in God which asks no proof ("You shall not put the Lord your God to the test."), and a dedicated allegiance to him which excludes all lesser claims ("Do homage to the Lord your God and worship him alone."). Surveying the career of Jesus as it appears in the gospels, we can see that these were the keynotes of the whole.

The account of the "testing" could no doubt have been compiled retrospectively out of such a survey. But we have good reason to believe that Jesus had in fact faced his test and made his decision before ever he came out in public. In one of his parables he observes, "No one can break into a strong man's house and make off with his goods unless he has first tied the strong man up; then he can ransack the house." [8] The implication is not far to seek: he had himself tied the strong man up; he had cleared scores with the devil before his work began, and he could carry his campaign into the enemy's country unhampered by any indecision or uncertainty about either his ends or his means. It is not at all incredible that he himself depicted the conflict and its issue in some such dramatic and symbolic form.

What followed? Mark, having briefly summarized the story of the "testing," takes a leap forward: "After John was arrested, Jesus came into Galilee." But where was he in the meantime, and what was he doing? Mark did not know, or was not interested. Nor was Matthew, and Luke was not aware that there was any interval at all. John, however, reports that Jesus was for a time at work in Judaea, administering baptism to the people who came flocking to him, and this seems credible. Apparently he had decided that he could not do better for the time being than second the efforts of the Baptist and carry forward the work of preparation, waiting for a sign that it was the will of God for him to take a more decisive initiative. During this time he would appear to the public as an ally, or even a lieutenant, of the Baptist—or perhaps a rival, and a successful one. This success, John hints, was unwelcome in some quarters: "A report now reached the Pharisees, 'Jesus is winning and baptizing more disciples than John.' When Jesus learnt this, he left Judaea and set out once more for Galilee." [9] It may be true that the suspicious interest which the authorities in Jerusalem were beginning to show was one consideration pointing to a new departure. But it is likely that the thing that decided him was, as Mark says, the arrest of John.

The Baptist, it appears, had gone a step too far in criticizing the irregular matrimonial arrangements of the local princeling, Herod Antipas, who thereupon clapped him in prison (at the fortress of Machaerus, Josephus tells us, near the Dead Sea), and there he was afterwards put to death. But Josephus also tells us something else: "Herod was terrified of John's influence with the people. He feared it might lead to an uprising, for they all seemed ready to do anything at his instigation. So he thought it much better to forestall any subversive action he might take, and get rid of him." Without necessarily denying the motive of private pique that Mark alleges, we may be fairly sure that political considerations were not far from Herod's mind. The gospel writers, understandably, tend to play down this aspect of the situation, but we ought always to keep in mind the

chronic political instability which was an inseparable part of the background.

However that may be, the mission of John the
Baptist was thus brought abruptly to a close, and
this, it seems, was for Jesus the sign he had been
awaiting. The work of preparation was over. He
came into Galilee proclaiming, "The time has come;
the kingdom of God is upon you."

Galilee was to be the base of operations for the
campaign which was now launched. How long it
continued to be so we do not know. Nor does the
silence of Matthew, Mark and Luke rule out the
possibility, or even the likelihood, that the Galilean
mission was from time to time interrupted by visits
to Jerusalem. A point came later, at which there was
a definite shift to the south, but at the start Galilee
was the principal terrain. The movement of events
cannot be reconstructed in detail; the necessary evidence is not available. But according to the general
run of the gospel narratives Jesus was during this
period engaged in three main types of activity, two
of them arising out of his deliberate plan, the third
forced upon him.

First, he was engaged upon a broad appeal to the
public, by way of addresses in synagogues, preaching
in the open air, teaching when he could find an
audience willing to listen, and discussion with members of the public who wished to raise questions.
The themes he dealt with we have already reviewed.
His master aim was to make people aware of the
presence of God as an urgent reality, and to induce
them to give the appropriate response, so that they
might become effectively members of the new people
of God which was coming into being.

Secondly, he set himself to minister to human need
by healing the sick in body or mind, by awaking

faith in those who had lost hope or the courage to
live, and by leading people, one by one, into a new
life under the inspiration of a personal attachment
to himself.

The two kinds of activity which we have noted—
the public appeal and the service to individuals in
need—run together. The spirit by which both are
pervaded is nowhere more forcibly expressed than in
one of the best known of the poetical utterances reported in the gospels:

> Come to me, all whose work is hard, whose load
>   is heavy,
>   and I will give you relief.
> Bend your necks to my yoke and learn from me,
>   for I am gentle and humble-hearted;
>   and your souls will find relief.
> For my yoke is kindly, my load is light.[10]

The call is public, addressed to all who will hear;
the response is necessarily made by individuals. The
deep compassion that breathes through it is unmistakable, but no less strongly marked is the note of
authority. Jesus lays a "yoke" on his followers; but
it is *his* yoke, and unlike the "yoke of the commandments" of which the rabbis spoke, it is a "kindly"
yoke. Paradoxically, the yoke and the load bring
"relief" to burdened souls. Pursue the paradox, and
it brings us somewhere near to the secret of what
Jesus was doing.

The third kind of activity which bulks largely in
the accounts of his work in Galilee is controversy.
This was something which Jesus did not seek, at this
stage. It was forced upon him. In the pursuit of his
mission he found himself obliged not merely to
neglect some of the finer points of current religious

practice (such as fasting on the proper days) but also to break some of the rules which were thought necessary to safeguard the religion of the Law (such as those of sabbath observance). Whether his actions did in fact amount to breaches of the Law in its true intention was arguable, and he did argue it. But they looked ill in one who set up as a religious teacher. Still more open to misconstruction was his evidently deliberate effort to cultivate friendly relations with classes of people from whom it was a point of honor to hold aloof. He risked incurring guilt by association. Not only so, he sometimes took upon himself to assure these people that their sins were forgiven, and that seemed unpardonable presumption, if not something worse. On all these points he was subject to criticism, and found it necessary to defend himself.

Added to all this, it seems, was an uneasy suspicion aroused by his remarkable healing powers. Evidently these could not be simply denied. If his critics were not prepared to admit that they betokened "the finger of God," there was (in their view) only one alternative. They challenged him to produce a sign from heaven to prove that his powers came from God, with the implication that if he failed to do so they would draw their own conclusions.[11] He refused brusquely to do anything of the kind. The inference followed: "He drives out devils by the prince of devils"; in other words, he was a sorcerer. According to Jewish tradition (as we have seen) this was one of the charges on which he was condemned to death. In the gospels it appears rather as a "smear" than as a possible ground for criminal proceedings, but it was dangerous all the same.

A milder form of this "smear," perhaps, represented him as simply out of his mind, and his own relations either suspected that this was the truth or at least thought it wise to put him under some restraint until the ugly rumor should blow over. With this intention his mother and brothers tried to approach him. But he could not now submit to the claim of the family, though this claim was a binding one in Jewish society. When later on he gave the warning that anyone who joined him must "hate" father and mother, he knew what he was talking about. The new community which was forming around him must henceforth be his family: "Here are my mother and my brothers; whoever does the will of God is my brother, my sister, my mother." [12] As the breach with his relations foreshadows the tragic separation from his whole nation which was to be his fate, so his new "family" is the nucleus of the emerging people of God.

How soon the forces of opposition gathered against him it is difficult to say. It may be that the gospels, with their abridged and selective report, have made it look a swifter process than it really was. At any rate it is clear that his mission won a substantial measure of success, so far as success can be gauged by vast audiences, wide notoriety, and an excited following. But Jesus himself was less than satisfied with the response he got. At his home town, we are told, "he was taken aback by their want of faith." [13] "A prophet," he commented ruefully, "is without honor in his own country." [14] He bitterly lamented his failure in the Galilean towns where he was chiefly active, Capernaum, Bethsaida and Chorazin. What he missed in these towns was repentance, a change of heart, as at Nazareth he missed faith. Popularity, it seems, was his for the asking, but not faith, and not repentance, on anything like the scale he desired; and popularity, as we shall see, had its drawbacks.

Yet it was not all failure, by any means, even by the standards by which Jesus reckoned success; so much is clear. A considerable number of Galileans did respond and become disciples, in the sense that they adhered to him personally and were guided by his teaching, though not necessarily giving up their ordinary avocations to stay in his company. Out of this body an inner circle drew together. They accompanied Jesus on his journeys and put themselves at his disposal. At a certain stage of his mission he brought them into active service by sending them out to carry abroad his own message, "The kingdom of God is upon you." The intention seems to have been to face as many people as possible with the challenge inherent in that proclamation.

I have described it as a recruiting campaign; not of course that Jesus was persuading people to "join," or entering names in a list of members. But in a sense already explained he was recruiting for the new Israel. At the same time there was another movement bidding for support—the national liberation movement of the Zealots. Its back had been broken, militarily, some years earlier, and it had gone underground. For the time it remained, so far as we know, without organization or leadership, but sporadic outbreaks proved that its force was far from spent. A favorable public for its propaganda was found in Galilee, and particularly among the humbler orders of the populace there. This was just the public to which Jesus at this time was appealing. Up to a point they seemed to speak the same language. The Zealots, as Josephus tells us, refused to recognize the Roman government because "they held God to be the only Governor and Master," and rather than acknowledge any man as master they endured indescribable sufferings. [15] This sounds not unlike th~

kingdom of God with its demand for exclusive loyalty. The two movements were likely to come into
contact, perhaps into competition. And in fact one
Zealot at least passed into the other camp and entered
the inner circle of the disciples of Jesus.[16] We may
be sure that there were others with a Zealot background among the wider body of adherents. After
the death of Jesus, so Luke relates, one of those who
had followed him said wistfully, "We had been
hoping that he was the man to liberate Israel." [17] It
is likely that many others thought he might turn out
to be the national liberator.

All this has to be kept in mind as we approach an
episode in which, it would appear, the work of Jesus
in Galilee found its culmination, and its virtual conclusion.[18] The disciples whom he had sent out recruiting returned from their tour—or perhaps from
the latest of such tours—with a gratifying success
story. But it seems that Jesus was not altogether easy.
He proposed that they should retire to "some lonely
place where you can rest quietly." Perhaps the need
for rest was not the only motive for temporary retirement. They took boat across the lake, only to find
their purpose foiled. They were faced with a vast
concourse gathered in the open country, to the esti-
mated number of four or five thousand. Jesus saw
the crowd, we are told, "like sheep without a shepherd," a leaderless mob without a clue. He had
meant to avoid an encounter like this, at that moment. But when he saw them "his heart went out to
them." So Mark, adding, "and he had much to teach
them." We conceive him reasoning with them, ex-
plaining himself, and trying to get them to see what
he stood for, all day until evening.

What happened then is one of the most puzzling
stories in the gospels. It must have had an important

place in the tradition, for not only is it reported in all four gospels, but two of them, Matthew and Mark, give duplicate accounts, differing unimportantly in detail. Briefly, we are told that Jesus fed the whole crowd on five loaves and two fishes (or alternatively on seven loaves and "a few" fishes). None of the attempts to make the story intelligible or credible by rationalizing it seem to carry conviction. But it may usefully be observed that the incident as it is presented to the reader is, primarily, not so much a miracle as a mystery. We are not told that they were "amazed," "astonished," or "dumbfounded" (which is the usual way of drawing attention to a miracle), but that "they had not understood." [19] John, after his manner, has appended a long discourse in which the mystery is expounded. The discourse is a series of variations on a theme; and the theme is drawn from the memory of that last supper at which Jesus broke bread for his disciples with the words, "This is my body" (which John gives, translating the Aramaic somewhat differently, as "The bread which I will give is my flesh"). He wishes us to see in the meal of the five thousand a prototype of the sacramental meal in which Jesus gave himself to his disciples, and which was perpetuated in the early church's rite of the breaking of bread. In the earliest order of service for such an occasion one of the prayers runs, "Thou, almighty Master, didst create all things for thy name's sake, and didst give food and drink to men so that they might give thee thanks. But to us thou hast given spiritual food and drink and eternal life through thy Servant." [20] This is the meaning that John intended this story to convey to his readers, and in Mark too the form in which the crucial part of the proceedings is related is so like the language

of his account of the last supper that a similar meaning is suggested.

But this does not necessarily dispose of the question, what was the place of this episode in the development of the mission on which Jesus was engaged.
The gospels treat it as in some way symbolic of
more than appears on the surface. It was a "sign,"
John says. From that it is an easy transition to the
hypothesis that Jesus himself intended it as such.
Nor is this at all a farfetched supposition. The Hebrew prophets who were his predecessors were accustomed to perform symbolic actions to reinforce
their words—"acted parables" as they are sometimes
called. Jesus did the same upon occasion. What was
there, then, in the event of that memorable day to
give it a symbolic value? First of all, to break bread
together is in all societies a token, and an instrument,
of community. Secondly, we know that Jesus made
use of the image of a feast to signify the blessings
of the kingdom of God consummated in a world
beyond this. He also hinted in parable that these
blessings were even now available: "Come; everything is now ready," is the message that the host
sends to his invited guests in one of his stories.[21] We
might fairly assume that a whole day's teaching had
not omitted the theme of the kingdom of God and
its present reality. Luke in fact says that this was the
subject of his teaching on this occasion. And when
at the close of the day the feast was spread, it was
not difficult to read in it the proclamation, "The
kingdom of God is upon you. . . . Come; everything
is now ready." Thirdly, Jesus was himself the host.
"I did not come," he had said, "to invite virtuous
people, but sinners," [22]—and here he was doing it.
The long day of teaching, culminating in the impressive symbolic action, may have been something

like a last appeal to the Galileans to understand and embrace his true purpose. It failed, just as the mission to Nazareth had failed to evoke "faith," and the mission to Capernaum, Bethsaida, and Chorazin had failed to evoke "repentance."

The response was disconcerting. Jesus became "aware that they meant to come and seize him to proclaim him king." In that brief phrase John passes over what must have been a gravely critical situation. It was no less than an attempted rising against the government with Jesus as leader. If he had been a "Messiah" of the common sort it was a golden opportunity; but that sort of messiahship he had long ago rejected as a temptation of the devil. It remained to put an end to a situation which threatened to compromise his whole mission. First, the disciples must be isolated from dangerous contacts. He "compelled" them, Mark says (as if they were reluctant to leave the exciting scene), to take to the boat and cross the lake—and that at nightfall and with a storm brewing. Then he used his remaining influence with the crowd to induce them to disperse peaceably, and retired in solitude to the hills.

So read, the narrative fits aptly into its place in the turbulent history of first-century Palestine. As the church moved outwards and made its appeal to wide circles in the Graeco-Roman world, who could not have cared less about the internal tensions of that distracted country, the political side of the story lost interest. It was forgotten except in one branch of the tradition, that followed by John. What remained was the memory of a sense of baffling mystery at the center of the whole transaction. The mystery concerned the action of Jesus in giving bread to the hungry crowd. Something about the way he gave it seemed to remove his action from the cat-

egories of everyday experience: "they did not understand about the loaves." It was one of the many
question marks which (as the gospels credibly inform
us) things that Jesus said and did imprinted on the
minds of his followers. Only the remoter sequel
would bring an answer to the question. The three
earlier gospels get little further than a naive wonder
that so little should have fed so many. John knows
the answer at which the church arrived after much
pondering in the light of later experience: "I am the
bread of life." [23]

VIII

THE STORY:
(II) JERUSALEM

AFTER THE DRAMATIC scene which we have just been considering, the gospels begin to introduce a fresh series of place names, which seems to indicate an expansion of the area of movement. Any attempt to plot out a detailed itinerary would be an unhopeful project. Our information is fragmentary, and not easy to combine into an intelligible whole. There is little to suggest any further activity in Galilee, at any rate on the scale or in the manner of earlier days. We hear of journeys outside Jewish Palestine, and of activity in Transjordan, as well as on the borders of Samaria, which lay south of Galilee on the west bank. Some of this probably belongs to the period after the crisis in Galilee, but we cannot be certain.

There are, however, some probabilities. It is clear that after the encounter with the five thousand patriots things could never be the same again, and it is no surprise when Mark tells us that Jesus withdrew for a time into foreign territory. No doubt opposition had been hardening in the synagogues, stimulated by the "doctors of the law who had come down from Jerusalem." There was reason to apprehend hostility from Herod Antipas, whose domain included Galilee; at some point (but we do not know when) Jesus received a warning that Herod was out to kill him, as he had killed John the Baptist.[1] But to all appearance it was less the threats of the opposition than the misguided enthusiasm of would-be followers that recommended a temporary retirement from the scene. Things had reached such a pass that any further public appeal in Galilee was inadvisable for the present. A new strategy would have to be worked out.

The fiasco of the abortive rising, we are told, had resulted in widespread desertions. From John's account we might gather that no followers at all were left except the faithful twelve. But he does not actually say so, and the extent of the defection need not be exaggerated. In any case, for any new departure at this point Jesus must rely on the more intimate group of fully committed disciples, whose loyalty was certain, and who at the same time were capable of being led into better understanding of what he was about. These he led across the frontier, out of Herod's domains, out of the restrictive atmosphere of the synagogues, and away from the ferment of an over-excited nationalism. The journey into foreign parts was in no sense a mission to the heathen; Jesus wished to remain incognito, so far as this was possible for one of his notoriety. His chief preoccupation was the instruction of the disciples who accompanied him. This concentration upon a select group must not be misunderstood, as if he had given up the idea of the new Israel as an open society, and now restricted its membership to a holy remnant. As the sequel shows, he had by no means abandoned the appeal to the people at large, but it had now to be

made on different lines; the part which the Twelve
were to play in it was one which would try them
more severely; and for this they had to be schooled.

But we should probably conceive this time of retirement in part also as giving Jesus himself an opportunity of seeing more clearly how he was now to
proceed in fulfillment of his vocation. Its main lines
were fixed from the time of testing which followed
his baptism; but the kind of action it called for at
any given stage must be determined by developments
in which he read the signs of the divine will for his
guidance. Between his baptism and his irruption
into Galilee with the proclamation of the kingdom
of God, as we saw, he had marked time, until the
removal of John the Baptist gave the signal for
advance. So now, we may suppose, developments in
Galilee having closed one door, he had to find out
in what way the next step should be taken. Exactly
how his mind worked we cannot pretend to know,
but two things come out clearly: the objective is to
be Jerusalem; and to go to Jerusalem is to face a
violent death. The two themes are inseparable in a
whole cluster of sayings which are so placed in the
gospels as to prepare the reader for the account of
the last journey and its tragic outcome.

If the mission of Jesus had as its aim the integration
of a new Israel as the true people of God, then sooner
or later his message must be presented, and presented
in a way that challenged a decisive response one way
or the other, at Jerusalem, the central hearth and
shrine of historic Israel. The time came when he
saw clearly that this would cost him his life. Such
was his assessment of the situation, based, we must
suppose, on an interpretation of various significant
incidents, some of them recorded, others unknown
to us.

He is unlikely to have arrived at this shattering conclusion without having been at Jerusalem to see how things were shaping. Mark indeed (followed by Matthew and Luke) has so concentrated attention on the final, and fatal, visit to Jerusalem as to give the impression that he had never previously visited the capital since his public activity began. But an attentive reading between the lines may suggest otherwise. At any rate even Mark's narrative presupposes that when he entered Jerusalem for the fatal Passover he already had friends and adherents in the neighborhood. John has a circumstantial account of a visit at the Feast of Tabernacles, which fell between the middle of September and the middle of October, some six months before the Passover at which he was to meet his death. He went up, John says, "not publicly, but almost in secret," as if he wished to observe without being observed, taking the temperature of feeling in metropolitan circles.[2] But "when the festival was already half over" he was moved to address the crowds in the temple.[3] What he said so incensed them that he was in danger of being lynched.[4] In the Fourth Gospel this episode is made, after John's manner, the setting for a whole series of dialogues and discourses which are evidently his own composition, though they contain undoubted reminiscences of earlier tradition, but there seems no valid reason to reject his statement that in September or October Jesus was in Jerusalem, and that the reception he met with finally convinced him—whatever premonitions he may previously have entertained—that any advance on the city would meet with implacable hostility. But go to Jerusalem he must. "It is unthinkable," he said with mournful irony, "for a prophet to meet his death anywhere but in Jerusalem."[5]

This, then, was the way in which the mission of the Servant of the Lord was to be consummated. This was how the ideal of self-sacrifice was to be translated into brute fact. Pointers afforded by the outward course of events coincided with the inner promptings of his vocation: he must go to Jerusalem—and die there. From this point on his actions are those of a man who knows that his life is forfeit, and is indifferent to whatever his enemies may do.

When he broached his plan to his closest followers, Peter's immediate reaction, as we saw, was to repudiate the whole idea as an unfortunate aberration. But loyalty to the Leader prevailed, and, though without any clear understanding of what was happening, they steeled themselves for the ordeal, and followed him. Mark portrays the mood in which the march began: "They were on the road, going up to Jerusalem, Jesus leading the way; and the disciples were filled with awe; while those who followed behind were afraid." He had timed his approach to Jerusalem for the season of Passover, in March or April. It was a time when masses of pilgrims from all over the Jewish world would be present, and his challenge could be delivered with the widest publicity. Moreover, the festival commemorated the liberation of Israel from Egypt—the birth of the nation. This year's Passover was to be marked by its rebirth as the true people of God. The setting for the challenge to Jerusalem was eminently appropriate.

How the interval between October and April was occupied or where it was spent we could only conjecture; the differing accounts of the various gospels at this point are hard to correlate. When we are able to pick up a straightforward narrative again the party have just crossed from Transjordan to the west bank; the halting places are Jericho and Bethany, both on the road between the fords of Jordan and Jerusalem.

It is at this point that signs of prior planning begin to appear. So far, it is assumed, Jesus and his company had traveled, as usual, on foot, but when they reached the outer suburbs he called a halt, and (says John) "found a donkey and mounted it." The other gospels suggest that it was not quite so casual as that. Mark has a circumstantial story (copied by Matthew and Luke) about the way the donkey was "found." Apparently it had been left "tethered at a door outside in the street" at the entrance to the village (presumably either Bethany or the neighboring Bethphage), ready to be released to messengers who gave the password, "Our Master needs it."[7] There is nothing improbable in the story, if we assume that Jesus has been in Jerusalem and its neighborhood before, and made contacts there; and there is good reason for believing that he had. Even if (with many critics) we should reject the story as picturesque embroidery, there seems no reasonable doubt that Jesus did ride into Jerusalem on a donkey. It is unlikely to have been a mere matter of convenience. It may best be understood as one more symbolic action, or "acted parable," after the manner of the prophets. What was its significance we may perhaps best ask after looking more closely at the incident itself.

We have to imagine Jesus and his party as traveling in company with large numbers of other pilgrims making for Jerusalem. Among them would be many Galileans. It would appear (in this all gospels are agreed) that Jesus had not been much in Galilee of late, or, if there, not much in the public eye. As he now rode conspicuously among them, his Galilean fellow-pilgrims greeted him with enthusiasm. John may well be right in saying that other pilgrims who

had arrived at Jerusalem in advance now heard of his
approach and came out to meet him. The last mile
or so turned into something like a triumphal procession. "Blessings on him who comes in the name of
the Lord!" they shouted. But cheers were also heard
for "the coming kingdom of our father David," and
these were ominous. They recall all too clearly some
of the poetry of militant nationalism which was current.

> Behold, O Lord, and raise up their king, the son
>   of David,
>   at the time thou hast appointed, O God,
>   to reign over Israel thy servant.
> Gird him with strength to shatter wicked rulers.
>   Cleanse Jerusalem from the Gentiles who tram-
>   ple it and destroy.
> In wisdom, in justice, may he thrust out sinners
>   from God's heritage,
>   crush the arrogance of the sinner like a potter's
>   crocks,
>   crush his whole substance with an iron mace,
>   blot out the lawless Gentiles with a word,
>   put the Gentiles to flight with his threats! [8]

Read "Romans" for "Gentiles" and the contemporary relevance of this warlike hymn becomes plain.
The man on a donkey does not easily fit into the picture. His strange entry into the city reminded
Matthew and John of a prophecy in the Old Testament. As quoted by Matthew it runs, "Tell the
daughter of Zion, 'Here is your king, who comes to
you in gentleness, riding on an ass,'" The prophet
continues his description of the gentle king: "He
will cut off the chariot from Ephraim and the war-
horse from Jerusalem, and the battle bow shall be
cut off, and he will speak peace to the Gentiles." [9]

As we might put it, he will carry out a program of disarmament and, instead of declaring war on the Gentiles, or "putting them to flight with his threats," he will make overtures of peace to them. If we suppose Jesus to have had this prophecy in mind, then his decision to enter the city in this guise is explained. He was challenging the people to rethink their ideas and their hopes for the nation: "Look on this picture, and on that!" The alternatives were before them.

Arrived in Jerusalem, he made his way, like most pilgrims, directly to the temple. But for the moment he did no more than look around and take note of what he saw with a view to future action; so at least Mark has it. Then he returned to Bethany for the night. Next morning he was back in the city, prepared to carry out an action designed to be the central point of his challenge to priests and people. It was to be staged within the temple precincts. The outer court was in these weeks before the festival the scene of a market where animals and birds could be bought for sacrifice, and where pilgrims from abroad could change the money they brought with them into currency acceptable for religious dues and offerings. The market was at least countenanced by the priesthood. The temple area was their special domain, its guardianship their exclusive responsibility. Jesus now ordered the traders to leave the place, overturned the tables at which currency transactions took place, and drove out the beasts. He then took control and prevented traffic from using the sacred precinct as a short cut. It was undeniably a highhanded action. It was also a bold one. The priests had a police force at their disposal, and in the castle that towered over the temple area a Roman garrison kept watch. The expulsion must have been effected with a minimum of disorder, and we cannot but conclude that the force which effected it was simply the personal authority that made itself felt when Jesus confronted the crowd. Many of them are likely to have sympathized with his action; others perhaps were overawed. There can hardly have been any conspicuous resistance, or the garrison must have intervened to forestall a riot; it was what they were there for. Jesus took command, and, for the moment, he was obeyed. Making the most of the opportunity he had thus made for himself, he spent the rest of the day teaching the people, who, Mark says, were "spellbound by his teaching." Of its content we are told very little, but perhaps enough to give a pointer to one at least of its themes, as well as to the purpose and meaning of his drastic action.[10]

It was not intended as a *coup d'état,* for he took no steps to follow it up. It must have been something in the nature of a manifesto in action. For its significance we must follow any clue that the gospels provide. But first we may note that the very fact that the temple was chosen as the stage for this demonstration made it clear at once that his aims, though he had been acclaimed as a king, were not political; it was the worship of God, not the independence of the Jewish state, that he was concerned with. "Do not turn my Father's house into a market." With these words, according to John, he expelled the traders, asserting the elementary principle that the worship of God and the pursuit of gain—and even of funds for religious purposes—are two things and not one. "You cannot serve God and Money," as he had observed earlier. So much is on the surface, but there is more beneath. One of the ancient prophets—the same, indeed, who spoke of the "king coming in gentleness"—also drew a picture of a good time to come

when men of all nations will go up to Jerusalem to
worship the King, the Lord of hosts; and on that day,
the prophet adds, "there shall no more be a trader
in the house of the Lord of hosts." [11] Jesus was offering symbolically a fulfillment of that prophecy, in
line with his basic affirmation that the kingdom of
God is here. So at least John understood the scene,
and such an understanding coheres with the general
tenor of the gospels.

In Mark (followed by Matthew and Luke) the
traders, or rather their priestly patrons, are accused
of having turned the temple into a "robbers' cave"
—not a "den of thieves"; that expression, which has
passed from the King James Version into our current
speech, is a mistranslation. The Greek language has a
word for "thief," derived from a root which connotes
something underhand, furtive, crafty; but that is not
the word used here. It is a different word, which primarily connotes not larceny but violence, and was
appropriately used of a highway robber or a gang-
ster. The caves of the Judaean wilderness had long
been the strongholds of these miscreants, and of the
revolutionaries who were scarcely distinguishable
from them, and were called by the same term. The
charge that Jesus brought against the traders is not
one of sharp practice in business, though with such a
valuable monopoly in their hands they perhaps did
not waste the opportunity. The charge is that the
priesthood was exploiting the sanctity of the temple
to make it the stronghold of a powerful and exclusive
faction, whereas it was intended to be "a house of
prayer for all nations." [12] So a prophet had declared
some centuries earlier:

As for the foreigners who adhere to the Lord to
worship him, to love his name, and to be his serv-

ants . . . I will bring them to my holy mount and
make them joyful in my house of prayer. Their
sacrifices and offerings shall be accepted on my
altar, for my house shall be called a house of
prayer for all nations.

In the prophet's own day it was a protest against the
morose exclusiveness which was the dark side of the
Jewish reformers' zeal for religion. As such Jesus
took it up. We recall that the Son of David was popularly expected to "cleanse Jerusalem from the Gentiles." Jesus wanted it cleansed *for* the Gentiles.

It was on the occasion of this "cleansing," according to John, that Jesus used the words which gave so
much offense: "Destroy this temple, and in three days
I will raise it again." As we saw, the temple is here
a symbol for a way of religion and a community embodying it, and the saying is a veiled forecast of the
emergence of a new Israel out of the corruption of
contemporary Judaism. In the light of this, the
"cleansed" temple becomes itself a symbol of the
new order, in which there is no distinction of Jew
and Gentile, but a united people of God offers him
a pure worship "in spirit and in truth" (as John puts
it elsewhere). A symbol, but only a symbol: the true
temple, "not made with hands" (as Mark has it), was
yet to come into being. The crisis out of which it
would emerge was now impending. The demonstration in the outer court was one more link in the
chain of events which brought Jesus to his death—to
his death and to his resurrection, which was also, in
his mind, the rise of the new people of God embodied in him.

It was not to be expected that this open challenge
to the priestly custodians of the temple should pass
unnoticed by them. "By what authority are you

acting like this?" they asked. "Who gave you this
authority?" [13] It was quite in character for Jesus to
meet such a question by asking another. He reminded them of his predecessor, John the Baptist:
Was he a prophet sent by God, or only one more
sectarian leader? This touched a sore point; the
official representatives of Judaism had been suspicious of the Baptist's goings-on, and yet in view
of his immense influence with the people at large
they did not care to repudiate him in express terms.
"We do not know," was the lame reply. "Then,"
Jesus retorted, "neither will I tell you by what
authority I act." The implication is that there is a
kind of authority which is self-authenticating; either
you recognize it or you don't, and if you don't there
is nothing more to be said. The reference to John
the Baptist is not a mere debating point. His work
had been one of the "signs of the times" in which
Jesus saw tokens of the coming of the kingdom of
God, and in accepting baptism at his hands he had
embraced his own vocation. John's program, "to prepare a people fit for the Lord," set the course which
Jesus had followed. John's assault on the complacency of official Judaism had sounded a note
which Jesus echoed. John had said (negatively)
that Jewish descent was in itself no qualification for
membership in the new Israel; Jesus now said
(positively) that the new temple should be for all
nations. He was asking the priests to recognize, be-
latedly, that the movement which John had initiated
and he himself had carried into a new phase, was
a work of God. The appeal found no response.

The priests were right in seeing that by his action
Jesus had raised the issue of authority. The foundation on which the Jewish establishment rested was the
assumption that supreme and unquestionable author-

ity resided in the Law of Moses and could be rightly
exercised only by the governing body believed to be
in true succession to the lawgiver. At any rate it
could be exercised by them alone "until" (as some
said) "a faithful prophet should arise"—one who
would hold authority direct from God who gave the
Law. Could Jesus be recognized as holding such
authority? Were they to look on while he exercised
it? It would mean abdication.

Jesus now passed from defense to attack. He appeared publicly in the temple and, in the presence
of large audiences, delivered trenchant criticisms of
the official representatives of the Jewish religon. The
sharp point of his attack is to be found in a parable
which reads almost like a declaration of war.

> A man planted a vineyard and put a wall round
> it, hewed out a winepress, and built a watchtower;
> then he let it out to vinegrowers and went abroad.
> When the season came, he sent a servant to the
> tenants to collect from them his share of the prod-
> uce. But they took him, thrashed him, and sent
> him away empty-handed. Again, he sent another
> servant, whom they beat about the head and
> treated outrageously. . . . He now had only one
> to send, his own dear son. In the end he sent him.
> "They will respect my son," he said. But the ten-
> ants said to one another, "This is the heir; come,
> let us kill him, and the property will be ours." So
> they seized him and killed him, and flung his body
> out of the vineyard.[14]

Like other parables, this one depicts an incident such
as might well have taken place in the existing situation, when growing popular discontent might at any
time erupt in open violence. Like others, it invited
the hearers to a judgment: "What will the owner of

the vineyard do?" Obviously it could be nothing short of a termination of the tenancy and the re-letting of the property. "They saw," says Mark, "that the parable was aimed at them." They must indeed have done so, if they were not peculiarly dim-witted! The prophets had spoken of Israel as God's vineyard. The religious leaders of Israel knew that they were there to manage it for him. They understood the parable, rightly, as accusing them of gross abuse of their position and, in effect, serving notice of dismissal on them in the name of the Owner; the vineyard would be let to new tenants. In other words, Israel is still the Lord's vineyard, but the existing establishment is doomed; the new Israel will be under different leadership.

Such is the dénouement of the parable, and such its inevitable application. But the gradual unfolding of the plot—the fruitless dispatch of messenger after messenger and their sinister reception—has also its own significance, That God had sent "his servants the prophets" to Israel, generation after generation, to remind them of their obligations to him, was an established part of the interpretation of their history which all Jews were taught. How Jesus thought about the sad story comes out in another saying of his which would seem to belong to the same situation of acute tension, though its tone is more that of regret than of denunciation:

> O Jerusalem, Jerusalem, the city that murders the prophets and stones the messengers sent to her! How often have I longed to gather your children as a hen gathers her brood under her wings; but you would not let me.[15]

The religious leaders, then, can hardly have missed the general purport of the parable, but it must have left them with a question in their minds: if the Owner's servants are God's messengers the prophets, who is the final messenger whose tragic fate is the climax of the story? Who is the Owner's son? It might imply a dangerous claim.

Matters now moved fast. The priests had evidently decided that Jesus was too dangerous a person to be left at large. John indeed has a circumstantial account of a meeting of the great council which resolved on his death. The discussion, he says, was opened by a speaker who drew attention to the influence which Jesus was exerting on the public, and the danger that his activities might lead to a move by the Roman authorities which might be disastrous to the Jewish community. The debate was wound up by the high priest Caiaphas, who stated the case bluntly as he saw it: "It is more to your interest that one man should die for the people than that the whole nation should be destroyed." [16] In the nature of the case this cannot be taken as anything like "minutes of the proceedings," but there is little doubt that it accurately puts the case as the priests saw it. Jesus must be "liquidated" to avert the danger of disturbing the extremely delicate balance by which Judaea enjoyed a limited autonomy under Roman rule. It seemed to the council that there was here sufficient ground for action; at any rate they could put him under arrest, and that was an action which the governor might be expected to countenance, since it could be represented as being in the interests of public order.

If the authorities were to act, they must act quickly, if possible before Passover, which was now very close at hand. The city was already filling up with pilgrims. Many of these might be found to sympathize with Jesus, and if an attempt were made

L

to arrest him publicly they might well riot in his support, and bring about just that military intervention
which it was the object of the exercise to avert. Jesus,
well aware of the danger, was now taking care not to
be found in the city after nightfall; he either stayed
with friends at Bethany or bivouacked on the Mount
of Olives, where the little company would easily
escape notice among the numerous groups which
camped out there for the festival. The projected
arrest, therefore, was quite a problem. An unexpected
solution now presented itself. One of the twelve disciples who were nearest to Jesus was found to be
willing to assist the authorities in effecting a secret
arrest.

The motive which led Judas Iscariot to an act
which has made his name a byword for the basest
treachery is probably beyond discovery. Matthew
indeed has a circumstantial story of his driving a bar-
gain with the priests, and he even knows the exact
amount of money that changed hands. But here
we may reasonably suspect a certain amount of
embroidery, the more so since Matthew has also an
edifying story about the traitor's remorse and grisly
end—a story, by the way, inconsistent with another
account of his death which is found in the Acts of the
Apostles, not to mention a third divergent account
which we know to have been handed down tradi-
tionally in the early church. It was natural enough
that legend should have grown about this monstrous
piece of treachery. Mark and Luke say simply that
Judas approached the priests with an offer to betray
his Master, and that they thereupon promised to
pay him for his services. John knows nothing of any
financial transaction. He says, as does Luke, that the
act of Judas was inspired by the devil; that is to
say, it was a piece of sheer irrational evil, the motive

for which was beyond their comprehension; and that is probably as much as they knew about it. No doubt money may have passed, but it was unlikely that so human, if so sordid, a motive as plain avarice had much to do with it. In the unsavory ranks of traitors to their country who have been exposed in recent years it seems that, while in most cases some consideration was offered and accepted, there were few for whom gain was the dominant or sufficient motive. Some deep-seated psychological maladjustment, a chip on the shoulder, thwarted ambition, misdirected idealism—these and other motives were at work. It would not be difficult to imagine ways in which some such motive might have influenced Judas, given his background and the situation in which he now found himself. But all this would be mere guesswork. We don't know; nor probably did those who first told the gospel story. "The devil put it into the mind of Judas son of Simon Iscariot to betray him"; [17] that is about as far as we can get.

The way was now clear, and the priests could go ahead with their plan for a speedy and secret arrest. One evening in that week Jesus and his twelve disciples met, with due precautions, at a house in Jerusalem where a room had been privately reserved for him, we may surmise by a sympathizer who did not wish to come out into the open (there were probably many such). Here they had supper together, for the last time, as it turned out. And indeed the air was heavy with forebodings. This was no ordinary meal. Although the day was perhaps not the official date for the celebration of Passover (it is known that the official calendar was not universally observed at this time), yet for them is was (or else it took the place of) the solemn Passover supper; and the historic memories which the festival recalled were present to their minds, arousing the deep emotions with which these memories were laden. But the words and actions of Jesus gave a new significance to the occasion. There were bread and wine on the board; of the profound meaning which Jesus attached to the breaking of the bread and the sharing of the cup something has already been said, and need not be here repeated.

Supper over, the company left the house and made for a familiar spot, an enclosure on the slopes of the Mount of Olives, across the valley from the east gate of the city. Judas Iscariot had already slipped away, on some errand, it was supposed, which fell to him as treasurer of their modest common fund. The others seem to have been in a mood of mingled exaltation and bewilderment; they felt they were in the midst of momentous happenings, but had little inkling of the real nature of the crisis that was upon them. "Pray that you may be spared the hour of testing," Jesus said. He himself was not to be spared. "Horror and dismay came over him, and he said to them, 'My heart is ready to break with grief.' " [18] So Mark has written, for once permitting the language of emotion to breach the severe reserve of his narrative. Jesus now left his friends and withdrew "about a stone's throw," to fall into solitary and agonized prayer. After some time he rejoined them, calm and resolute. "Up, let us go forward; my betrayer is at hand." And even as he spoke, lights were seen among the olive trees, and a posse of armed men approached, with the traitor Judas at their head. There was a brief attempt at resistance, but Jesus quickly put a stop to it and gave himself up. The disciples scattered, and Jesus was in the hands of his enemies.

The arrest had been effected, as the priests had de-

sired, without attracting attention or giving any opportunity for a rescue by possible sympathizers. The
Prisoner was now to be brought to trial. In the
account of the proceedings given in the gospels we
have, in appearance, reports of two separate trials,
one before a Jewish court, the other before the
Roman governor, each ending in condemnation on
a capital charge—but a different charge in each. We
have to bear in mind the ambiguous standing of the
Jewish council, the Sanhedrin. In its own estimation
it was the sovereign assembly of the nation of Israel,
with authority to administer the law delivered by the
Almighty to Moses on Mount Sinai, from which
there was no appeal. In cold fact, Judaea being a
Roman province, it was a municipal organ of administration, with powers just as wide as Rome
allowed, and no wider. Under the liberal policy of the
empire, which allowed a fair degree of local autonomy, the Sanhedrin exercised wide jurisdiction as a
court of justice, especially in matters arising out of
the peculiar practices and institutions of the Jewish
religion. But the governor had ultimate responsibility. In particular, he kept in his hands all cases
involving a capital charge. This was a principle in
force throughout the empire. The only known ex-
ceptions, where a local court had the power of life
and death, were a very few free cities, incorporated
in the empire by treaty, not by conquest. Jerusalem
was certainly no free city, and there is no sufficient
evidence that the Sanhedrin enjoyed any such improbable privilege. It may, on occasion, have acted
ultra vires, and a governor may have saved himself
trouble by looking the other way; some such apparently irregular cases are cited. But in the case of
Jesus of Nazareth there were reasons why no ir-
regularity must appear.

The priests had a double aim in view: Jesus must be removed by death; he must also be discredited. The death sentence therefore must be legally and formally pronounced by the governor. The surest way to secure such a sentence would be to cite the Defendant on a charge of political disaffection. But such a charge would by no means discredit him in the eyes of the Jewish public; quite the contrary. It was for the Sanhedrin to show that he was guilty of an offense against religion. The prestige of the court would secure respect for the verdict. Yet in fact the Sanhedrin could act only as a court of first instance. And that is what the gospels say it did. Although the council appears to have pronounced the Prisoner guilty and liable to the death penalty, the priests came into the governor's court, not as judges seeking confirmation of their verdict, but as prosecutors. So the gospels all agree. The proceedings before the council therefore take on their proper character as a preliminary investigation to determine the charge to be preferred before the competent tribunal. Such was the legal position, though in the eyes of orthodox Jews the judgment of the native court was valid in itself, and Jewish tradition in the Talmud assumes that the death sentence was passed by the Sanhedrin; understandably, it ignores the role of the governor altogether.

The arrest had been made at dead of night. Naturally, the council was not in session. But one man at least was awake; and expecting the result: Annas, the *éminence grise,* no longer High Priest, but lurking formidably in the background, while his son-in-law Caiaphas discharged the sacred office by grace of Pontius Pilate. Before him the Prisoner was immediately brought for private and informal questioning, "about his disciples and about what he taught." So John (alone among the gospels) reports, noting that a disciple of Jesus who was acquainted with the High Priest had found his way into the house—which we may possibly take as a hint that he had good information at this point.[19]

Meanwhile, we must suppose, steps were being taken to acquaint members of the Sanhedrin with the successful arrest and to secure a full attendance at a hastily summoned meeting. It must have taken some time, and we should probably accept Luke's statement that the full session, with the High Priest himself presiding, took place in the morning. This would bring it into conformity with the rules of procedure, as they are known from Jewish sources. If the session was held at night, as might appear from Matthew and Mark, then the strict provisions of the Law were infringed, and by the High Priest himself. Perhaps they were, but it is more likely that the writers of the gospels have telescoped events. They were not concerned with nice points of legal procedure, nor indeed with chronological precision. Their narrative faithfully portrays the movement of the drama, with its fundamental unity and continuity, even though in fact the interval between the arrest and the session of the council, and between that and the trial before Pilate, may have been more considerable than appears.

The account of the hearing before the Sanhedrin is not without difficulties. The reports in Matthew and Mark (variants of the same) differ in some points from Luke's, and John does not report the hearing.[20] At best we are at a disadvantage in having no more than a very brief *précis*, in Greek, of proceedings conducted in Hebrew, which may have been quite lengthy. Mark's account is fullest. He indicates that the object was "to find some evidence against Jesus

to warrant a death sentence," and this is probably
not far from the truth. But the forms of law were
scrupulously observed. Several charges were preferred, of which Mark specifies only one, that of a
threat to destroy the temple. This was a perversion of
something which Jesus had actually said, as we have
seen. But the witnesses could not agree upon the
form of words they professed to have heard, so the
charge lapsed. It was a principle of Jewish law that
the evidence of "two or three witnesses" was required
for a conviction. Nor did the other charges find the
necessary consentient evidence. Nevertheless Jesus
was offered the opportunity of replying to them,
which he declined. The High Priest then interrogated him directly: "Are you the Messiah?" Here
serious difficulties begin, for, as we have seen, the
gospels do not entirely agree about the reply he gave.
In any case, the High Priest construed it as a confession that he did make such a claim. Not only so;
he gave it as his opinion that the words used were
blasphemous. The court unanimously concurred, and
the Prisoner was convicted of blasphemy, a capital
offense in Jewish law.

Wherein the "blasphemy" consisted it is not easy
to say. It is not clear that a claim to messiahship was
in itself necessarily blasphemous. Presumably the
offense lay in the implications of the language used.
Elsewhere in the gospels the charge of blasphemy is
particularly associated with two matters in which
Jesus gave offense to Jewish religious feelings: he pronounced the forgiveness of sins,[21] which seemed to
mean usurping the divine prerogative of judgment,
and he "called God his own Father" (as distinct from
the sense in which he was the Father of all Israelites).[22] There may be an echo of both in the language
used in the account of the interchange between the

High Priest and his Prisoner. Jesus was asked, not
only whether he was Messiah, but whether he was
the Son of God. In Mark the two are combined, but
in Luke he is asked first, "Are you the Messiah?" (to
which there was no reply), and then "Are you the
Son of God?" (to which he replied, "It is you who say
that I am"—a noncommittal answer capable of
being construed as an admission). It looks as if the
expression, "Son of God," was not treated as a simple
synonym of "Messiah," but was understood to be
loaded (as Jesus used it) with startling implications.
And these seemed to be emphasized when he went on
to speak of "the Son of Man seated at the right hand
of God," and associated this with the antique vision
of final victory, in which "one like a son-of-man" is
invested with universal sovereignty. If it appeared
that in speaking of the Son of Man he was referring
to himself, which (as we saw) would be consistent
with common usage of language, then there might
well seem to be here matter of blasphemy, in the
sense of an outrageous affront to the most deeply
held beliefs and sentiments of the Jewish religion.
Whether it could be brought under any statutory
definition of the crime is a question to which we have
not the material for an answer. And indeed in what
I here put forward there is already some reading between the lines. At any rate, the upshot of the investigation was that Jesus stood before the Jewish
public tainted with a crime at which they shuddered.
But Caiaphas had also succeeded in finding a charge
which could be brought before the Roman court; for
"Messiah" could readily be translated into "king of
the Jews" and that was something that the governor
could not ignore. Of the charge of blasphemy we hear
nothing further; that was something of which the
Roman court could not take cognizance.

Jesus, then, was cited before the prefect on the charge of claiming to be "king of the Jews," or, in other words, of being a leader of rebellion against the emperor. There were possibly two supporting charges (so at least Luke says, and he may well be right) : subverting the people, and forbidding the payment of tribute. These perhaps were stock charges against a nationalist agitator. The case therefore was presented as political from first to last, without any ostensible religious overtones. There is no improbability in the impression which the gospels convey that the prefect would have been glad to decline jurisdiction, as he could have done if the charge were reduced, or modified, so that it would come within the competence of the Jewish court. Matthew indeed has a dramatic scene in which Pilate calls for a basin of water and publicly washes his hands. Perhaps we should not take this as matter of fact, but that the prefect would have liked, meta-phorically, to "wash his hands" of the affair is credible enough. He had learned by bitter experience how easy it was to fall foul of the susceptibilities of his incalculable subjects. But if the priests insisted on the capital charge he was bound to proceed with it.

The temperature of national feeling was always high about the Passover season, and it was hardly ex-ceptional that at this very time there had been dis-turbances which called for police action. Three "bandits" (as the gospels call them, using the official term for what we might call "freedom fighters") were in custody awaiting execution, among them their leader, one Barabbas. And now the governor was asked to deal with another prisoner, Jesus of Naza-reth, who (so the priests alleged) claimed to be king of the Jews. Was he, then, perhaps the real ring-leader? What evidence was offered we are not told,

nor are we informed in detail about the course which
the interrogation of the Prisoner took. It has been
reduced to the simple question, "Are you the king of
the Jews?" to which, according to all gospels alike,
Jesus gave the noncommittal reply, "The words are
yours." John adds that he put in a plea in his defense: he could not be regarded as a leader of revolt,
because he had no followers in arms. Since John
himself says that the examination was held *in
camera,* he can hardly have known exactly what was
said. But the defense would have been a valid one,
corresponding with the facts, and Pilate could easily
have drawn the inference for himself, that, whatever
may have been intended by the claim to royalty
(which Jesus did not disown), the Prisoner was not
a danger to the state. If so, that would account for
his reluctance to convict, in spite of a *prima facie*
presumption of guilt involved in the claim itself.

Moreover, **Pilate** had formed the impression that
Jesus was a popular figure. So, as a conciliatory
gesture to the populace—and perhaps also as a snub
to the priests, whom he obviously disliked and
despised—he offered to give the Prisoner an uncon-
ditional discharge. But he had miscalculated. "Not
this man; we want Barabbas!" the crowd shouted,
incited, we are told, by the priests. Nowadays we
know all too well how easily a "spontaneous" popular
demonstration can be staged by interested parties,
and the clamor for Barabbas need not be given more
weight than this. But the prefect was driven into a
corner. When he still hesitated, the priests played
their trump card: "If you let this man go, you are
no friend to Caesar." The implied threat is obvious.
Pilate had already more than once put himself in the
wrong with the local authorities, and had reason
to fear what in fact happened in the end, when he

was recalled to Rome to answer their complaints before the emperor. He dared not oppose their wishes
any longer. After all, the Prisoner had made a tech-
nically treasonable claim which he refused to deny
when given the opportunity, and the law must take
its course. So sentence of death was pronounced.[23]

Jesus was led to the place of execution in the
company of two of Barabbas' desperadoes—three
"bandits" to be punished for their crimes by Roman
justice was what the public was intended to see. All
three were crucified, after the brutal Roman practice.
No fouler or more agonizing form of torture, perhaps, has ever been devised. The day wore on; Jewish law required that the bodies of the crucified
should be removed before Sabbath began at sunset.
Jesus was found to be already dead; his fellow
sufferers were dispatched. His body was saved from
the indignities commonly reserved for executed
criminals, and he was given decent, though hasty,
burial through the good offices of a well-to-do sympathizer. After sunset, the people of Jerusalem, and
the numerous pilgrims up for the feast, turned to
the celebration of Passover; for this was the day set
for it in the official calendar.

IX

THE STORY:
(III) THE SEQUEL

THE STORY AS TOLD in the gospels does not end with Jesus dead and buried. They go on to say that he had risen again.[1] That this was so is a conviction that runs through the whole of the New Testament. As I said earlier, it is not a belief that grew up within the church; it is the belief around which the church itself grew up, and the "given" upon which its faith was based. So much the historian may affirm. Can he go further and ask what actually happened to give rise, or to give tangible form, to such a belief?

Our gospels never set out to *describe* the resurrection of Jesus Christ as a concrete occurrence (though some apocryphal gospels do). The question with which we should approach them is, how did his followers, who knew that he had been put to death by crucifixion, come to be convinced that he was still alive? To this question they give two answers: first, that the tomb in which the body of Jesus had been laid was subsequently found empty; and secondly, that he was seen, alive after death, by a number of his followers.

First, then, all four gospels report that on the

Sunday morning after the Friday on which Jesus had died his tomb was found to be vacant. The discovery was first made by a woman follower of his known as Mary of Magdala, either alone or in the company of other women, all of whom had been present at his death. So far all gospels agree.

Luke adds that the discovery was afterwards confirmed: "Some of our people went to the tomb and found things just as the women had said." John particularizes: the persons in question were Peter and another disciple. The condition in which they found the tomb, described in meticulous detail, confirmed, and more than confirmed, what Mary had told them; and they "saw and believed." The story is told with the dramatic realism of which this writer is master. It looks like something as near first-hand evidence as we could hope to get. Perhaps it is, and if so, it becomes the sheet anchor of belief in a "bodily resurrection." But the relation between seeing and believing is one of John's favorite themes; and at this point he is preparing the way for the pronouncement in which his gospel, as originally designed, found its climax and conclusion: "Happy are those who did *not* see and yet believed." Is he, then, here constructing an "ideal scene" in which the conditions for belief as based on "sight" are as favorable as they could possibly be, only to suggest that such belief is not, in the end, the most important or permanent kind of faith? It may be so.

At any rate it is remarkable that this is the only place in the gospels where the belief that Christ had risen is a direct inference from observation of the state of the tomb. In Matthew and Mark an angel assures the women, "He is not here; he has been raised again." In Luke, "two men in dazzling garments" make a similar announcement. In the Bible, where angels are introduced, it is very often an intimation that a truth is being conveyed which lies beyond the reach of the senses, a "revelation." We might think of a discovery made (there are many such on record) by an imaginative, or "inspired," leap beyond the immediate data, to be verified by subsequent experiment. On this analogy, what the women saw brought only perplexity; then, by a leap beyond the evidence of the senses, they knew what it meant. But it still awaited verification from later experience.

It is indeed upon this verification that all the gospels lay stress. They seem unwilling to rest their case on negative testimony ("They *failed* to find the body," as Luke says), and they tend in a curious way to minimize it. According to Mark the women "said nothing to anybody" about what they had seen. According to Luke, they did report to the disciples, "but the story appeared to them to be nonsense, and they would not believe them"; nor does he suggest that the confirmatory visit brought any more positive conviction. According to Matthew, the women were on the way to report when Jesus met them—and this was news better worth the telling. In John, Mary, finding the tomb laid open by the removal of the covering stone, concludes without investigation that the body has been removed by some person or persons unknown, and reports to the disciples in that sense, but as in Matthew, a meeting with Jesus himself resolves all uncertainty. The writers were evidently aware (perhaps they had learned by experience in trying to win credence for their message) that the mere fact that the tomb appeared to be untenanted, even if it were accepted, would not necessarily prove their case. The body might have been removed by friendly or by unfriendly hands; [2] both possibilities are allowed for (only to be refuted, of course). In any case the tendency is to shift the emphasis from the evidence of the empty tomb to the personal encounter with Jesus.

Elsewhere in the New Testament the evidence of the empty tomb is never adduced, though most of its writers have much to say about the resurrection of Christ. But an examination of the language they use may show that it implies more than we might suppose. It is true that they sometimes express their belief in such noncommital phrases as "Christ died and came to life again," [3] or, "In the body he was put to death; in the spirit he was brought to life." [4] But far more frequently they use such expressions as, "He rose from the dead," or, "He was buried; on the third day he was raised to life." The natural implication would be that the resurrection was (so to speak) the reversal of the entombment. The same implication seems to emerge from a careful reading of some other passages, though it may not be on the surface. Passages such as I have cited can be traced back to a time well before the composition of the gospels. It seems hard to resist the conclusion that this is how the early Christians, from the first, conceived the resurrection of their Lord. When they said, "He rose from the dead," they took it for granted that his body was no longer in the tomb; if the tomb had been visited it would have been found empty. The gospels supplement this by saying, it *was* visited, and it *was* found empty.

In Jewish circles at the time, those who believed in a life after death at all seem mostly, though not universally, to have imagined it as some kind of resuscitation of the body which was buried. Is it possible, then, that the earliest Christians, convinced on other grounds that Jesus was still alive, gave expression to this conviction in an imaginative or symbolic form suggested by the common belief, and that this was the origin of the story in the gospels? It may be so. Or, again, it may not. As we have seen, the story about the women at the tomb, on the showing of the authors themselves, circumstantial as it is, remains inconclusive as evidence apart from further verification. It looks as if they had on their hands a solid piece of tradition, which they were bound to respect because it came down to them from the first witnesses, though it did not add much cogency to the message they wished to convey, and they hardly knew what use to make of it.

I should be disposed to conclude that while the general tradition held that Christ "rose from the dead" (commonly understood to mean that he emerged from the tomb in which his body had been laid) it preserved also a genuine memory that on that Sunday morning his tomb was found broken open and to all appearance empty. At first the discovery was disconcerting and incomprehensible; later it was understood to mean that Jesus had in some way left his tomb. Whether this meaning was rightly attached to it, and if so in what sense, is another question, and one which lies no longer in the sphere of the historian. He may properly suspend judgment.

The main weight, in any case, is placed on the testimony that Jesus was "seen," alive after death, by a number of his followers, and here we are on firmer ground. We may start with the earliest known recital of the facts.[5] This takes us back a long way behind the gospels. It is cited in one of the letters of Paul. Writing about a quarter of a century after the death of Jesus, he says that the tradition passed on to him, presumably when he became a Christian

M

some twenty years earlier, contained the following statements: "that Christ died; that he was buried; that he was raised to life on the third day; and that he appeared to Cephas and afterwards to the Twelve. Then he appeared to over five hundred of our brothers at once, most of whom are still alive, though some have died. Then he appeared to James, and afterwards to all the apostles." On these facts, he says, all Christian teachers are in full agreement, whatever differences of opinion there may be about other matters.

It is apparent that Paul sets store by the consensus, as evidence for the *facts:* if anyone doubts, he is free to interrogate those whom he mentions. They include Peter (Cephas), the leading member of the most intimate circle of the disciples of Jesus, and James, his own brother. Paul knew them well. He had met them both, and spent a fortnight with Peter, when he visited Jerusalem a very few years after Jesus was crucified—almost certainly not more than seven years, possibly no more than four. We have here, therefore, a solid body of evidence from a date very close to the events. Something had happened to these men, which they could describe only by saying that they had "seen the Lord." This is not an appeal to any generalized "Christian experience." It refers to a particular series of occurrences, unique in character, unrepeatable, and confined to a limited period.[6]

It is with this background in mind that we should read the reports of the appearances of the risen Christ in the closing pages of the gospels. One thing the attentive reader will notice at once: the continuous narrative which ran from the account of the entry into Jerusalem to the discovery at the tomb is now broken. We have something more like a number of detached incidents. It is true that Luke and John show some ingenuity in weaving the incidents they relate into a single story, but the result looks artificial, and in any case it is not the *same* story. We have the impression that the occurrences described were not of a kind to enter into a developing narrative. They were sporadic, elusive, evanescent, yet leaving in the minds of those to whom they happened an unshakable conviction that they had indeed, for a short space of time, been in the direct presence of their living Lord.

The incidents are reported in stories of various types, some concise and almost bald, stating the bare minimum of fact, some told at length with deliberate artistry. But the pattern of all is the same: the disciples are "orphaned" (the phrase is John's) of their Master; suddenly he is there—it may be in a room, on the road, in a garden, on a hillside, beside the lake, wherever they happen to be. At first there is amazement, with some doubt or hesitation (sometimes made explicit, always perhaps implied), and then, with overwhelming certainty, they recognize him. In Luke, two travelers entered into conversation with a stranger on the road; he sat down to supper with them, and suddenly "their eyes were opened and they recognized him." In Matthew (whose account is much more formalized) the disciples in Galilee were aware of a presence which some of them recognized at once, "but some were doubtful"; then he spoke, and they knew perfectly well who it was. In John, Mary of Magdala, by the dim light of early morning, sees someone in the garden. She thinks it is only the gardener, but he speaks: "Mary." "My Master!" she replies. The fishermen in their boat on the lake after a disappointing night's work, catch sight of an unknown figure who hails them from the beach. He encourages them to make one more attempt, which

succeeds. "It's the Lord!" one of them exclaims—
and so it is. This is the dramatic motive of all these
stories. In almost all other particulars they differ, and
the attempt to harmonize them is not hopeful. In
describing occurrences which, *ex hypothesi*, lay on
the extreme edge of normal human experience, or
beyond it, the writers are hardly to be pinned down
to matter-of-fact precision in detail; and indeed the
accounts they give, taken literally, are problematic
if not contradictory. In various ways they are trying
to justify, even to rationalize, what was for the
original witnesses an immediate, intuitive certainty
needing no justification. They were *dead sure* that
they had met with Jesus, and there was no more to
be said about it. It was the recovery of a treasured
personal relationship which had seemed broken for-
ever. It was also, as we have seen, their reinstatement
after their failure in the "hour of testing." Now they
were new men in a new world, confident, courageous,
enterprising, the leaders of a movement which made
an immediate impact and went forward with an
astonishing impetus.

Clearly *something* had changed these men. They
said it was a meeting with Jesus. We have no evidence with which to check their claim. To propose
an alternative explanation, based on some pre-
conceived theory, is of dubious profit. What was the
nature of this meeting we cannot pretend to know.
What actually happened, if by that we mean what
any casual observer might have witnessed, is a question that does not admit of an answer. But the events
that make history do not consist of such "bare facts."
They include the meaning the facts held for those
who encountered them; and their reality is known
through the observable consequences. In this instance
we may be clearer about the meaning and the con-

sequences than about the "facts" in themselves, but this would be true of other momentous events in history. We are dealing with a truly "historic" event. It was the culmination of previous events in the lives of these men (summed up in their memories of Jesus), and the creative starting point of a new sequence of events of which the world was soon aware. It made them new men, but it was also the birth of a new community. Or rather, as they would have said, it was the rebirth of the people of God, the rising of Israel from the dead, and they were in it. It is because they speak out of the very center of this "new creation" that their witness carries weight. They themselves had passed through death to new life. The darkness and desolation of Good Friday and the miserable sabbath which followed it had emptied life of all meaning for them. On the "third day" they were "raised to life with Christ," as Paul put it; [7] and that is a confession of faith hardly less basic than the proclamation, "Christ is risen."

The "appearances" of the risen Christ, as we have seen, are represented as a series limited in time, and distinct from any subsequent type of "Christian experience." Luke, in his second volume (the Acts of the Apostles) has marked the close of the series by a symbolic scene in which, after "forty days" (a conventional number), Christ finally vanished from human view: "a cloud removed him from their sight." *That* chapter is closed, never to be repeated. But the entire New Testament is witness that the real presence of Christ was not withdrawn when the "appearances" ceased. The unique and evanescent meetings with the risen Lord triggered off a new kind of relation which proved permanent. The focus of this new relation is hinted at by John when he recounts how the risen Jesus gave bread to his disciples, and by

Luke when he says that he was "recognized by them at the breaking of the bread." Both writers, no doubt, are looking back to the words and actions of Jesus at his last supper, and both certainly have also in mind the "breaking of bread" which was the center of the Christian fellowship as they knew it, and remained so. In the fellowship the presence of the Lord no longer meant a sudden flash of recognition, utterly convincing but soon over. It was an enduring reality, creative of a new corporate life.

Within that corporate life, as it matured and expanded, and larger perspectives broadened out, their understanding of what had happened went deeper. It was not simply that their lost Leader had come back to them. God himself had come to them in a way altogether new. And that put the whole story in a fresh light. Matthew has made the point in the way he begins and ends his gospel. At the beginning he says that the true name of Jesus is Emmanuel, that is, "God with us." [8] He closes it with the words of the risen Lord: "I am with you always, to the end of time." [9] All that lies between, he means, is the story of how God came to be with men, for good and all. Starting from there the church embarked on the far-reaching intellectual enterprise which is the building of a Christian theology, and philosophy of life, upon the foundation thus laid. But that is another story, and it is not yet finished.

Notes and References

CHAPTER I

[1] Pliny *Correspondence with Trajan,* letter 96 (97).
[2] Tacitus *Annals* XV. 44.
[3] Babylonian Talmud. Tractate *Sanhedrin,* 43b.

CHAPTER II

[1] Luke 1. 1-2.
[2] Attempts which are made to show that Luke is based on Matthew (or, alternatively, Matthew on Luke) have not, in my judgment, succeeded. It still seems highly probable that both drew upon some common source, or sources, though few critics would now think it possible to reconstruct a supposed document containing all the common material.
[3] Specimens of early Christian preaching are to be found in Acts 2. 14-39, 3. 13-26, 10. 36-43, 13. 17-41.
[4] Acts 18.25.
[5] John 1.51.
[6] I have given reasons for this conclusion in *Historical Tradition in the Fourth Gospel,* pp. 21-136.

CHAPTER III

[1] Matt. 6. 25-29, Luke 12. 22-23.
[2] Mark 4. 26-27.

3 John 3.8.
4 Matt. 6.2.
5 Matt. 5. 23-24.
6 Matt. 7.3.
7 Luke 14. 8-11.
8 Matt. 5. 25-26, Luke 12. 57-59.
9 Mark 13. 24-26.
10 Mark 14.62.
11 Luke 10.18.
12 John 18. 15.
13 Matt. 11.19, Luke 7.34.
14 Mark 2.17.
15 Mark 9. 22-24.
16 John 5. 6-8.
17 Luke 19. 1-10.
18 John 7. 2-11. This passage was not originally part of the
   Gospel according to John, being absent from early
   manuscripts; but there is no reason to doubt that it
   was a genuine piece of tradition.
19 Luke 10. 25-37.
20 Mark 10. 17-25.
21 Mark 11. 27-33.
22 Matt. 8. 5-10, Luke 7. 2-9.
23 John 8. 28-29, 14.24.
24 Luke 12. 49-50.
25 Mark 9.19.
26 Matt. 11.27, Luke 10.22.
27 John 4.34.
28 John 16.32.
29 Matt. 26.39, Mark, 14.36, Luke 22.42, and compare John
   12.27.

CHAPTER IV

1 Matt. 11.25, Luke 10.21.
2 Mark 10.18.
3 Mark 10.27.
4 Mark 4. 28-29.
5 Matt. 13. 45-46.

[6] Matt. 5. 25-26, Luke 12. 57-59.

[7] Luke 16. 3-4.

[8] John 4.35.

[9] Luke 10. 23-24.

[10] Luke 16.16. Matthew's version of this saying is more enigmatic, 11. 12-14.

[11] Mark 1.15.

[12] Mark 6.15.

[13] Luke 11.20; Matt. 12.28 has the more conventional, "by the Spirit of God."

[14] John 12.31.

[15] John 3.19.

[16] Matt. 10.30, Luke 12.7.

[17] Luke 15.4.

[18] Matt. 7.11, Luke 11.13.

[19] Luke 15. 11-32.

[20] Luke 12.29, Matt. 6.32.

[21] Luke 11. 2-4; Matthew's longer version, 6, 9-13.

[22] Matt. 11.25, Luke 10.21.

[23] Matt. 18.3, Mark 10.15.

[24] Matt. 7.24, Luke 6.47.

[25] Matt. 22. 34-40, Mark 12. 28-34, Luke 10. 25-28.

[26] Matt. 23.23.

[27] Matt. 5.45.

[28] Luke 10. 29-37.

[29] Matt. 5. 43-48, Luke 6. 27-36.

[30] Matt. 5. 39-42.

[31] Matt. 18. 21-22.

[32] Luke 17.10.

[33] Matt. 6.15.

[34] Romans 11.22.

[35] Matt. 23.23, Luke 11.42.

[36] Mark 2.27, 3.4.

[37] Matt. 5. 21-22, 27-28.

[38] Matt. 12.35, Luke 6.45.

[39] Matt. 6. 1-6.

[40] Matt. 23.25, Luke 11.39, Mark 7. 15-23.

[41] Romans 14.14. Such is probably the meaning of the ex-

pression which is literally translated, "I know and am persuaded in the Lord Jesus."

[42] Luke 6.46, Matt. 7. 21-23.

[43] Mark 10.20, Matt. 19.20, Luke 18.21.

[44] Luke 18.9.

[45] Joseph Klausner, *Jesus of Nazareth* (English translation, 1925), p. 376.

CHAPTER V

[1] Horace *Odes* III. 5.

[2] Luke 19. 9-10.

[3] Luke 13.16.

[4] Matt. 15.24 (absent from some mss.).

[5] Matt. 16.3.

[6] Luke 13. 1-5.

[7] Mark 11.17.

[8] Matt. 3.9, Luke 3.8.

[9] This idea is elaborated into a highly dramatic picture in Ezekiel 37. 1-14.

[10] Luke 11.50-51, Matt. 23. 35-36.

[11] Luke 19. 41-44. The vivid details of the siege are drawn from descriptions of the siege and capture of Jerusalem by the Babylonians in 586 B.C.

[12] John 2.19, Matt. 26.61, Mark 14.58.

[13] Mark 4. 26-29.

[14] Luke 10. 2-3, Matt. 9. 37-38.

[15] Matt. 4.19, Mark 1.17, Luke 5.10.

[16] Matt. 13.47.

[17] Mark 2.22, Luke 5.38, Matt. 9.17.

[18] Matt. 19.28, Luke 22.30.

[19] Luke 12.32.

[20] Mark 10. 42-44, Matt. 20.2.

[21] John 13. 5-9.

[22] Luke 22.27.

[23] Luke 14. 26-27.

[24] Matt. 10. 37-38.

[25] Mark 10.38, Matt. 20.22.

[26] Mark 8.35.

[27] John 12. 24-25.
[28] I Corinthians 11.25, Matt. 26.28, Mark 14.24.
[29] The new covenant: Jeremiah 31. 31-34.
[30] John 21. 15-19.

CHAPTER VI

[1] John 20. 31. It seems clear that the Fourth Gospel as originally planned, ended here, Chapter 21 is an appendix.
[2] John 4. 25-26, in a private conversation with a Samaritan woman.
[3] Mark 8. 27-30, Matt. 16. 13-16, Luke 9. 18-21; and compare John 6. 67-69.
[4] Mark 14. 61-62, Matt. 26, 63-64, Luke 22. 67-70; and compare John 10.24.
[5] Mark 15.2, Matt. 27.11, Luke 23.3, John 18. 33-37.
[6] Mark 8. 31-33.
[7] The most important of these is the poem contained in 52.13—53.12, but the theme of the Servant is seldom long out of sight through chapters 40-55. The language of these chapters is echoed with remarkable frequency all through the New Testament, either in direct quotation, or by way of allusion. I have made a list of such echoes in *According to the Scriptures*, pp. 88-103.
[8] Isaiah 42. 1-4, quoted in Matt. 12. 17-21.
[9] Isaiah 49.5.
[10] Matt. 15.24: In Luke 19. 1-10 Zacchaeus is represented as just such a "lost sheep"; he is a "son of Abraham" who has strayed, and Jesus "has come to seek and save what is lost."
[11] Isaiah 53. 10, 12.
[12] Mark 10.45. This is no bad summary, in the fewest words, of what Isaiah said about the Servant of the Lord.
[13] Mark 1. 10-11; compare Matt. 3. 16-17, Luke 3. 21-22, John 1.32.
[14] Psalm 2. 7.

[15] Isaiah 42. 1.
[16] Isaiah 44.1, 21, compare 45.4, 48.12, 49.3.
[17] Matt. 4. 2-10, Luke 4. 2-12. The passages in Deuteronomy referred to are 6. 13, 16, 8.2-3.
[18] Matt. 25.40.
[19] Matt. 18.5, Mark 9.37.
[20] Matt. 10.40.
[21] Mark 10.39.
[22] I Corinthians 11.25, Mark 14.24.
[23] Mark 14.22, Matt. 26.26, Luke 22.19, I Corinthians 11.24, and compare John 6.51, which appears to be based on a different translation of the original Aramaic of the saying.
[24] I Corinthians 10.16, compare 12.27, Romans 12.5, Ephesians 4. 12, etc.
[25] It should perhaps be said that the view here put forward requires some modification of what I have previously written elsewhere. On the question of Aramaic usage I am greatly indebted to G. Vermes, in an appendix to M. Black, *An Aramaic Approach to the Gospels and Acts* (3rd edition, 1967) pp. 310-330.
[26] John 12.34.
[27] Mark 8.31, 9.12, 10.45, echoing the language of Isaiah 53. 3-5, 10, 12.
[28] John 16. 16-18.
[29] Matt. 16.27, Mark 13.26, Luke 17.24.
[30] Matt. 8.11, Luke 20.38.
[31] Matt. 25. 31-2.
[32] Luke 6.20.
[33] Mark 2.19.
[34] Luke 22.30.
[35] John12.31.
[36] Luke 7.50, &c.
[37] Matt. 11.24.
[38] Mark 14.62.
[39] Psalm 110.1.
[40] Daniel 7. 13-14, 18.
[41] Colossians 3.1.

CHAPTER VII

1 In this and the following chapters I have essayed an outline, and an interpretation, of the course of events, so far as this may be inferred from data in the four gospels. Inevitably this is to some extent conjectural. Informed conjecture, a legitimate tool of the historian, is often an indispensable tool to the historian of antiquity. For the result I do not claim more than a degree—as it seems to me a high degree—of probability.

2 Philip and Nathanael: John 1. 45-46.

3 I have attempted to put together such a "portrait" out of the parables in *The Authority of the Bible*, pp. 147-152.

4 A son learning his trade: John 5. 19-20a. Basically, this is a picture from daily life, but John, after his manner, has made use of it to enforce a theological point.

5 Josephus *Antiquities* XVIII, v.2, §§ 116-119.

6 John 1.26. The other gospels do not make this point, but it was most probably a part of the Baptist's message.

7 Mark 1. 12-13, Matt. 4. 1-10, Luke 4.1-13.

8 Mark 3.27.

9 John 3. 22-24, 4. 1-2.

10 Matt. 11. 28-30.

11 Luke 11. 15-16. Luke has seen that the demand for a "sign" and the accusation of sorcery belong together; in the other gospels they are reported separately, Mark 3, 22, 8.11. Matt. 12.24, 38, 16.1.

12 Mark 3. 21, 31-35.

13 Mark 6.6.

14 John 4.43, Mark 6.4, Matt. 13.57, Luke 4.24.

15 Josephus *Antiquities* XVIII, i. 6. § 23.

16 Mark 3.18.

17 Luke 24.21.

18 Mark 6. 30-44, 8. 1-10; Matt. 14. 13-21, 15. 32-39; Luke 9. 10-17; John 6. 1-15.

19 Mark 6.52, 8. 17-18, 21.

20 *Teaching of the Twelve Apostles*, 10.3.

[21] Luke 14.17.
[22] Mark 2.17.
[23] John 6.35.

CHAPTER VIII

[1] Luke 13.31. It was Pharisees who gave the warning; were they friendly? or was it an attempt to bring pressure to bear? One of the unanswered questions.
[2] John 7. 1-10.
[3] John 7.14.
[4] John 7.30, 8.59.
[5] Luke 13.33.
[6] Mark 10.32.
[7] John 12. 14-15, Mark 11. 1-10.
[8] The quotation is from the (so-called) Psalms of Solomon, 17. 23-27.
[9] Zechariah 9.9, quoted in Matt. 21. 4-5, John 12.15.
[10] Mark 11. 15-17, Matt. 21. 12-13, Luke 19. 45-46, John 2. 13-19. John has placed this incident at an earlier point, but this is dictated by the order of thought rather than by chronology. I have discussed it in *The Interpretation of the Fourth Gospel*, pp. 300-303, and *Historical Tradition in the Fourth Gospel*, pp. 161-162.
[11] Zechariah 14.21. The word translated "trader" could also mean "Canaanite," the Canaanites (known also as Phoenicians) being the great trading people of the Mediterranean; but the prophet has just invited "all the nations" to Jerusalem, and there seems no reason for a last-minute exclusion of the Canaanites.
[12] Isaiah 56.67, quoted in Mark 11.17. Matthew and Luke, in copying Mark, have left out "for all the nations," missing the point.
[13] Mark 11. 27-33.
[14] Mark 12. 1-12.
[15] Matt. 23.37, Luke 13.34.
[16] John 11. 47-53.
[17] John 13.2 and similarly Luke 22.3.
[18] Mark 14.34.

[19] John 18. 13-23.
[20] Mark 14. 55-64, Matt. 26. 59-66, Luke 22. 66-71.
[21] Mark 2.7.
[22] John 10. 33, 36, compare 5.18.
[23] Trial before Pilate: Mark 15. 1-15, Matt. 27. 11-26, Luke 23. 1-25, John 18. 28-29. 16.

CHAPTER IX

[1] The Resurrection narratives are in Matt. 28, Luke 24, John 20-21, and Mark 16. 1-8. In most of the ancient manuscripts the Gospel according to Mark ends with 16.8: whether he deliberately stopped there, or meant to write more but was prevented, or did write a conclusion which was afterwards lost, is an open question. The remaining verses are a later addition.

[2] By the gardener, Mary first thought; by the disciples, according to a Jewish rumor (Matt. 28. 13-15).

[3] Romans 14.9.

[4] I Peter 3.18.

[5] I Corinthians 15. 3-7.

[6] When Paul claims (I Corinthians 15.8) that he had himself "seen the Lord," after all the others, he admits that this was something unexpected, exceptional, and abnormal, an appendix to a series already closed.

[7] Colossians 3.1.

[8] Matt. 1.23.

[9] Matt. 28.20.